Contents

The pre-Conquest Civilizations

Olmec jade head. The pug nose, thick lips, slit eyes and puffy face are characteristic of all Olmec sculptures. The Olmec culture flourished in Mesoamerica from the twelfth to the second century B.C. (Museo Nacional de Antropología, Mexico City)

The discovery of the New World by Columbus in 1492 — probably preceded by Viking raids in the region of Labrador about A.D. 1000 — brought ruin upon the civilizations which had flourished up to that time in the vast territories of the American continents. The coming of the white man spelled disaster for both the Aztecs in Mexico, subjugated by Cortés from 1519 to 1549, and the Incas in Peru, pursued by Pizarro and his troops from 1524 to 1536.

Owing to a substantial technological lead (pyrometallurgy, firearms, oceangoing ships, cavalry, etc.), a handful of ruthless and intrepid adventurers intent on making a fortune crushed the magnificent pre-Columbian civilizations which fell into oblivion until Alexander von Humboldt originated American archaeology in the early nineteenth century.

The civilizations of pre-Columbian America evolved in total isolation. From the dawn of history till the Spanish Conquest they never once came into contact with other cultures or continents. The region was populated in the palaeolithic age by hunters who crossed over the Bering Strait, a land bridge between Asia and Alaska created by the lowered ocean level during early periods of ice formation over 40,000 years ago.

The American civilizations evolved quite independently from their Old World counterparts. The result was original and paradoxical, offering both enormous deficiencies and astounding discoveries. The pre-Columbians had no knowledge of the wheel, the plough or the potter's wheel; they had no domestic animals except dogs, turkeys and bees (as well as llamas in Peru); nonetheless they elaborated a system of writing and perfected astonishingly accurate calendars. Metallurgy was used only to produce sacred vessels for religious ceremonies and gold and silver ornaments. On the other hand, the pre-Columbians created vast political organizations and their societies were governed by powerful religious structures.

Pre-Columbian civilizations had an essentially agrarian economy. The main food crops were corn, sweet potatoes and black beans. They were however quite familiar with the properties of medicinal substances, spices and fibres such as cotton. Their total isolation from the rest of the world is proved by the non-existence of cereals (wheat or rice) in America before the Conquest as well as by the absence of cocoa, tomatoes, tobacco, quinine and cocoa in the Old World through the sixteenth century.

The Olmecs: the Mesoamerican Mother Culture

In this book devoted to the artistic, architectural and cultural achievements of the pre-Columbian world we shall focus our attention on the

THE PRE-COLOMBIAN CIVILIZATIONS
The World of the Maya, Aztecs and Incas

Text and photographs
by Henri Stierlin

SUNFLOWER BOOKS
NEW YORK

PRODUCED BY AGENCE INTERNATIONALE D'ÉDITION JEAN F. GONTHIER
8, avenue Villardin, 1009 Pully (Switzerland)

End papers:

The Palace of the Governors at Uxmal (Yucatan) built by the Maya in the eighth and ninth centuries is one of the master-pieces of pre-Columbian architecture in Mexico. The main structure is almost 60 m (197 ft.) long. In the foreground, the throne of the two-headed jaguar.

Title page:

Moche portrait-vase. The Classic Moche culture which flourished from the second to the seventh century in Pacific coastal Peru created admirable polychrome pottery. This moulded pot is an excellent example of the naturalistic Moche art style. (Musée d'Ethnographie, Geneva)

This edition published 1979 by Sunflower Books,
575 Lexington Avenue, New York, NY 10022, USA.

ISBN 0 8317 7116 x
Manufactured in Italy

THE PRE-COLOMBIAN CIVILIZATIONS
The World of the Maya, Aztecs and Incas

Olemc collosal head found at the site of La Venta (Tabasco). This enormous basalt monolith is 2.7 m (9 ft.) high and weighs over 20 tons. Stone was brought from quarries 120 km (75 mi.) away. (Villahermosa Open-air Museum)

Olmec altar found at the site of La Venta. A crowned figure sitting in a niche seems to peep from the open-fanged head of the jaguar worshipped by the Olmecs. (Villahermosa Museum)

7

main birthplaces of ancient American civilization: Mexico and Peru.

The Olmecs founded about 1200 B.C. the first great American civilization north of the equator. The Olmec heartland was southern Veracruz and western Tabasco, a region of swamps, lagoons and tropical forests along the Gulf Coast. In these luxuriant jungles ravaged by continuous flooding, the Olmecs, or "rubber people" — as they were named by their discoverers — erected vast ceremonial centres at Cerro de las Mesas, Tres Zapotes and La Venta. The architectural concept initiated at La Venta was to be followed at later sites throughout Mesoamerica. The most prominent feature of La Venta is a clay and earth pyramid 65 m (215 ft.) in diameter and 35 m (110 ft.) high. The leveled top probably supported a wooden shrine with a thatch roof. At the foot of this enormous mass the construction of which required 100,000 tons of building materials, two parallel 85 m (280 ft.) long sloping walls form the boundaries to a ball court. At the far end of the ball court were sacrificial altars and colossal sculptured basalt heads. These monolithic sculptures weigh over 20 tons each. The stone was brought from quarries 120 km (75 mi.) away.

This highly developed civilization seems to have emerged from prehistory already formed, just as Athena sprung already armed from Jupiter's brain. The Olmecs exerted the first culturally unifying influence on Mesoamerica. At their site of La Venta we find the two fundamental monuments which characterize the architecture of all later Mesoamerican civilizations: the pyramid, a raised platform constructed to support the temple, and the ball court. The ritual ball game was supposed to simulate the movement of the sun through the sky. The players used a solid rubber ball weighing over 1.5 kg (3.5 lbs.).

The wide influence of the Olmec civilization was not limited to the fields of architecture and site planning. Olmec myths and rituals were handed down to the Maya, Zapotecs, Mixtecs and Aztecs. The Olmecs were the first Mesoamerican people who invented a writing system. As early as 700 B.C. special hieroglyphics made it possible to record numbers and dates. Their complex calendrical concepts later appear in the culture of the Maya. The calendar elaborated by the Olmecs dates back to 3000 B.C. and is one of the most ancient known vestiges of Mesoamerican civilization.

Olmec clay baby figure dating from the first millenium B.C. Such figures with splayed legs are typical of the Olmec art style. (Museo Nacional de Antropología, Mexico City)

Large stone cage made up of basalt pillars. A live jaguar was probably kept in this strange construction found at the site of La Venta. (Villahermosa Museum)

8

Wrapped in the coils of an enormous serpent-dragon, a human figure wearing a helmet and holding a purse. This reptile is the earliest known effigy of the famous Quetzalcóatl, the Feathered Serpent god of the ancient Mexican pantheon. (Villahermosa Museum)

Olmec colossal head carved in basalt. These bodiless heads were placed like stelae at the foot of the clay and earth pyramid at La Venta. (Villahermosa Museum)

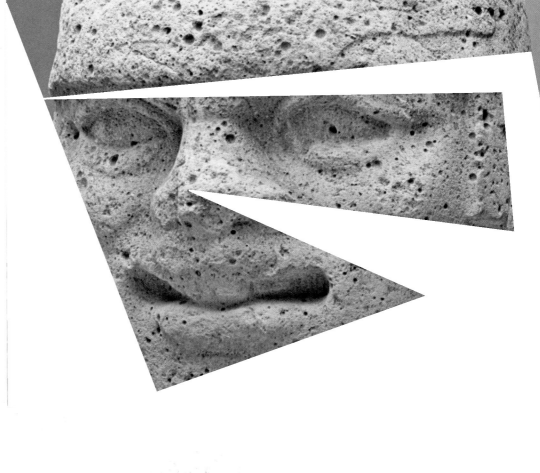

Classic Maya Ceremonial Centres

Maya civilization which may be compared to Greek civilization in the Old World was already on the wane in 1547 when the troops of Cortés took possession of Yucatán. The Yucatán peninsula is a strip of land which runs out into the Gulf of Mexico and separates the Gulf from the Caribbean Sea. Spanish conquistadores had great difficulties in clearing a way through the entangled jungle overgrowth which covers the lowlands, but they found it even more difficult to make their way into the southern provinces of high Maya civilization. This southern area overspread with dense rain forests comprises the highlands of Chiapas, Guatemala, Quintana Roo and westernmost Honduras.

Luxuriant forests cover not only the high plateaux but also the foothills of the volcanoes of Pacific coastal Guatemala. The Spanish conquerors found the ancient cities of the Maya Classic period drowned in an ocean of trees. These great ceremonial centres had been abandoned five hundred years before the first Europeans set foot in the land. Colonization cannot therefore be regarded as the cause of the downfall of this glorious civilization (indeed, Maya achievements in the arts and sciences surpass those of all other pre-Columbian cultures).

Roughly speaking, the two main regions comprised in the geographic scope of the Maya civilization — the southern area which includes the sites of Tikal, Uaxactún, Copán, Yaxchilán and Palenque, and the northern area with the sites of Uxmal, Kabah, Labná, Sayil and Chichén Itzá — were the scenes of two distinct cultural evolutions.

High Maya civilization began to flourish in the jungle of Petén about 1000 B.C. and experienced its fullest development from 200 B.C. to A.D. 700 which is known as the Early Classic period. The Late Classic period of the southern lowland Maya began in the seventh century of the Christian era and continued through the tenth century. Lowland Maya

Great pyramid at Tikal (Guatemala) facing the Great Plaza. This structure known as Temple I reaches a height of 47 m (154 ft.).

View of Temple II at Tikal from the raised platform of Temple I. Steep stairways lead to the shrine which crowns its four terraces.

civilization experienced a vigorous revival in 987 when the Toltecs invaded Yucatan. At Chichén Itzá monuments. In the twelfth century the centre of Toltec hegemony shifted to the fortress city of Mayapán which subdued the entire Yucatan peninsula until 1500 when the Spaniards arrived.

Although Humboldt was chiefly responsible for bringing the pre-Columbian world out of oblivion, the resurrection of Maya civilization which made the greatest contributions to Mesoamerican culture was largely due to the travel accounts of the explorer Stephens and his companion Catherwood who rediscovered the most important ancient sites about 1840. Rank jungle overgrowth had already invaded the Maya ceremonial centres and begun its work of destruction: temples attacked by tropical creepers, pyramids undermined by cedar and mahogany roots, stucco moldings eaten away by humidity, stelae overthrown, staircases broken asunder... Such was the sight that greeted the eyes of Stephens and Catherwood when they penetrated into the jungles inhabited by the Mayas' descendants, decimated by disease and malnutrition.

A century ago archaeologists began flocking to the major sites and long forgotten capitals of Maya civilization in the hope of restoring their ancient splendour. At many sites long years of patient labour have made it possible to rediscover the original appearance of Maya ceremonial centres. Anastylosis is rendered all the easier since these vast sacred cities lost in the heart of an impenetrable jungle were never resettled after their primitive inhabitants abandoned them a thousand years ago. The monuments have tumbled down but no extraneous elements have been added and modern archaeologists have but to put together the pieces of this gigantic puzzle.

Nonetheless, numerous problems remain to be solved before we will be able to re-create the primitive splendour of the palaces and temples, pyramids and ball courts abandoned by the ancient Maya. Specialists disagree about relevant criteria for establishing Maya chronology.

Group A facing the Great Plaza at Tikal is a complex structure made up of a series of shrines clustered about a rectangular court.

Above:
Maya stela at Tikal showing a high priest bearing the insignia of power.

Hieroglyphic writing has yet to be deciphered; up to the present only numbers and dates have betrayed their secret. Last but not least, the decline and downfall of these cities is still a puzzle to the experts.

A Great Religious Centre : Tikal

One of the most spectacular cities of high Maya civilization is doubtless Tikal (in modern Guatemala), a vast complex of monuments discovered by Gustav Bernoulli in 1877. Bernoulli was the first white man to set foot among the fallen splendours of this Maya ceremonial centre wrapped in a green shroud of jungle overgrowth. The low-relief which is now the prize archaeological exhibit at the Museum of Ethnography at Basle is a magnificent example of the art treasures of Tikal. In the twentieth century American archaeologists from the University of Pennsylvania undertook the enormous task of research and restoration which has made it possible for us to rediscover Tikal in all its original splendour.

The site of Tikal covers the same area as a modern town of 40,000 inhabitants. The most important monuments in the ceremonial centre are grouped about the North and Central Acropolis and the Great Plaza. High pyramids rise up above the tree-tops. Archaeologists have named them quite prosaically Temples I, II, III, IV and V. Steep stairways lead to the temples built on these raised platforms. The sanctuary proper is surmounted with a "cresteria", i.e. an ornamental superstructure in the shape of a stone crest which reaches a height of 45-50 m (150-165 ft.).

A flight of stairs leads up at a 60° angle to the tiny room suspended half way between earth and heaven which makes up the temple proper. The interior seems to be a replica of the huts which remain up to the present the principal dwelling-places of the numerous descendants of the lowland Maya. The vaulted stone roof is an imitation of traditional thatch roofing. Temple structure unquestionably represents a stone

Facing page:
The Temple of the Inscriptions at Palenque dates back to A.D. 692. The burial chamber of a priest-king was discovered in the heart of the pyramid.

Below:
Panoramic view of Palenque. To the left, the Temple of the Sun (A.D. 642). To the right, the multiple-court palace built in 672 with its square tower erected in 783.

One of the porticoes running along the façades of the Multiple-court palace at Palenque. Columns support a typical Maya corbeled vault.

copy of primitive Indian habitations. This phenomenon of petrification is characteristic of the entire history of pre-Columbian architecture.

Many Maya vaulted roofs have successfully withstood the assaults of the tropical forest which took possession of the abandoned cities over a thousand years ago. Some Maya temples have overhanging roofs with corbeled arches as for example at Copán. In others, well bonded fine limestone facing serves as a casing for concrete or lime mortar.

In some precincts of Tikal, platforms, small pyramids and palaces built on raised foundations with vast outer stairways are arranged after a manner resembling modern town-planning. The main features are a chequerboard layout and north-south site orientation. Public squares, inner courtyards and causeways set off the beauty of the monuments. Before building, Maya architects entirely reshaped the site and the surrounding landscape; this titanic feat necessitated the removal of more than ten tons of earth and rock. Since the wheel was unknown in Mesoamerica and the Maya had neither pack animals nor draught-animals, the colossal task was accomplished by human porters!

Stone stelae adorn the plazas. Stelae inscribed with Initial Series dates commemorate the date of the foundation of a monument or an important astronomical event. These columnar stone monuments are

decorated with hieroglyphic inscriptions and low-reliefs depicting noblemen and dignitaries in lavish attire. Most of these figures wear high feather head-dresses and jade jewelry. The cast of features is quite typical. Artists strongly emphasize the Maya profile, characterized by a curved, aquiline nose; the bridge of the nose juts out and forms a crest on the forehead.

Most of the pyramids and palaces at Tikal were built between the fifth and the eighth century of the Christian era. The "red stela", erected in A.D. 292, proves however that the site was an important religious centre long before that time.

An Important Discovery at Palenque

Among the great Maya ceremonial centres of the Classic period the site of Palenque stands in a class by itself. This complex placed in the foothills of the Chiapas Mountains overlooking the Tabasco plain was the scene of the most important discovery ever made in Maya archaeology. In November 1952 the Mexican archaeologist Alberto Ruz Lhuillier unearthed the famous tomb of the Temple of the Inscriptions: a genuine burial chamber hidden in the heart of the pyramid.

After patiently removing the debris obstructing a vaulted staircase

closed up by the architects after the funeral ceremony which took place about A.D. 633, Alberto Ruz discovered a chamber closed by a monolithic triangular door buried 22 m (72 ft.) beneath the pyramid's raised platform. When the door was opened, the astonished archaeologist penetrated into a splendid vaulted crypt where man had not set foot for thirteen centuries! The burial chamber housed an enormous carved memorial stone, 2 m (6.5 ft.) wide and 3 m (9 ft.) long, which weighed 8 tons. Under this memorial stone, a richly sculptured sarcophagus contained the remains of a Maya priest-king surrounded by countless jade ornaments and wearing a magnificent jade mosaic mask (the pre-Columbian Indians indeed believed jade to be more precious than gold).

This unexpected discovery created almost a big a stir as the discovery of Tutankhamen's tomb in Egypt thirty years before. It revolutionized archaeologists' hypotheses concerning Mexican pyramids. Specialists began to wonder if all were not tombs, as in Egypt. In actual fact, the existence of a sepulchre hidden in the heart of the pyramid is not uncommon in Maya ceremonial centres. Nonetheless, the pyramid's main purpose was to support the temple where religious ceremonies and sacrifices were performed. In Egypt, on the contrary, human beings were not allowed on the summit of the pyramid; the edifice's sides were moreover

Molded-stucco low-reliefs at Comalcalco recall the art style of Palenque. These sculptured figures bear witness to the admirable sensibility of Maya artists. The moustaches, slightly flaring lips, almond-shaped eyes, prominent bridge of the nose and diadem encircling the forehead are typical of Classic Maya works. The low-reliefs at Comalcalco rank among the masterpieces of pre-Columbian art. (Museo Nacional de Antropología, Mexico City)

Central court of the great palace at Palenque. The square tower in the background was probably an astronomical observatory. At the foot of the tower, a wide stairway lined with high stelae sculpted with human figures.

covered with smooth facing. In spite of the famous tomb discovered in the Temple of the Inscriptions, the Maya pyramid, constructed to support a temple, has much more in common with Mesopotamian ziggurats than with the gigantic sepulchres of Giza and Dahshur.

Another unusual feature of Palenque is the vast multiple-court palace erected in 672. The palace complex forms a rectangle made up of several freestanding edifices constructed on a steep raised platform. It includes long vaulted cloisters and lodgings reserved for the priests who governed the town. A three-storeyed square tower overlooks the palace complex. This structure built in 783 was probably used for astronomical observations.

The ceremonial centre at Palenque suffered greatly from the curiosity of the explorers who first rediscovered the site invaded by the jungle in the nineteenth century. In order to free the monuments from their leafy prison and unearth the treasures buried under luxuriant tropical vegetation, the explorers quite simply put fire to the forest. Such acts of vandalism damaged or destroyed many priceless works of art. The walls and roofs of the buildings were originally covered with an admirable molded-stucco relief decoration; the flames shattered the polychrome low-reliefs and made the corbeled arches collapse.

The site of Palenque is particularly renowned for its beautiful sculptures. Molded-stucco reliefs bear witness to the originality and high sensibility of Palenque artists. The portrait heads carved in the round discovered by Alberto Ruz in the crypt of the Temple of the Inscriptions rank among the finest masterpieces of the pre-Columbian world. Art style is astoundingly vivid and calls to mind the Amarna fashion in Egypt.

Such is the legacy of the splendid Maya ceremonial centres of the Classic period. The inexplicable decline of high Maya civilization began about A.D. 700–800.

The Magnificent Palaces of Uxmal

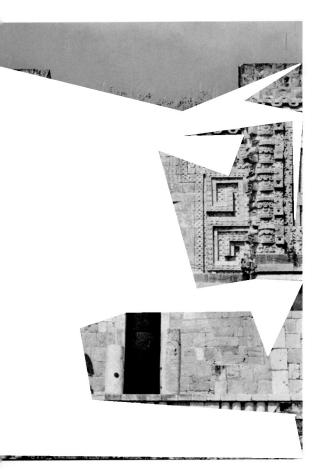

Palace of the Governors at Uxmal. Arcades with admirable corbeled arches connect the central building to the two wings.

Before the Classic period ceremonial centres of the southern area — Petén and the Usumacinta River drainage — were abandoned by their inhabitants, the Yucatán peninsula became the scene of the second zenith of Maya civilization. The architectural style which characterizes the monuments erected in the eighth and ninth centuries is quite different from that in vogue in the south.

The Puuc style is characterized by its purity of line, its modernism and its exuberant geometric friezes. Lowland Maya architects gave preference to long horizontal outlines; the palaces thus blend into the surrounding landscape.

Puuc architecture as seen at Uxmal, Labná, Kabah and Xtampak incorporated many aspects om the regional styles initiated at Río Bec and Chenes. The Puuc style drew inspiration from ancient traditions which find their roots at the site of Dzibilchaltún in northwestern Yucatán, occupied from 1000 B.C. to the present. Thousands of monuments were erected at Dzibilchaltún in the fifth century of the Christian era. Maya civilization actually evolved quite simultaneously in Yucatán and Petén.

Restoration of the Puuc Masterpieces

The flora of northern Yucatán is much less luxuriant than the rain forest of Petén with its high trees and humid undergrowth. The Northern Lowlands are a dry, wooded region. Trees are mostly deciduous and seldom reach a height of over twelve metres (40 ft.). Furthermore, rainfall is by no means as heavy as in the south. This explains why the monuments of Puuc architecture have been but slightly damaged by ambient nature. In Yucatán we find nothing similar to the destruction caused by the tropical rain forest at Tikal and Palenque.

Puuc sites such as Uxmal are generally well preserved and restoration is much less difficult than in the Maya southern area. In many cases the monuments are well nigh intact except for the wooden lintels surmounting palace doors which have collapsed. When these rotten timbers gave way, part of the stone mosaic frieze encircling the buildings also tumbled down. However, since these decorative bands were made up of identical mass-produced carved segments, one undamaged segment is sufficient to make restoration possible.

These architectural treasures have been rescued and preserved thanks to the efforts of the Mexican government. The palaces of Uxmal in particular are outstanding examples of Puuc architecture. This admirably beautiful and spacious palace complex was built by a civilization which had not yet come out of the Stone Age. Although the Maya produced a writing system, a highly accurate calendar and intricate mathematics, they made no use of bronze or iron. The splendid palaces of Uxmal were

Monumental stairway leading up to the Palace of the Governors at Uxmal, built between the seventh and the ninth century. The structure is decorated with a stone mosaic frieze. These three buildings with their haughty silhouettes and eleven doors look unbelievably modern.

Central hall of the Palace of the Governors. Three square doors open on to this area 20 m (66 ft.) long and 4 m (13 ft.) wide. The roof displays a typical Maya vault. The door to the left gives access to a dark narrow room.

19

Facing page:

Western stairway of the Pyramid of the Magician at Uxmal, leads to a temple which itself ressembles a mask.

Below:

Side view of the Turtle House at Uxmal. This austere structure is a perfect example of the Classic Puuc style.

Statuette found at Jaina. It portrays a Maya nobleman wearing a breastplate and a complicated head-dress. (Museo Nacional de Antropología, Mexico City)

built with the help of stone tools.

The Palace of the Governors at Uxmal (eighth-ninth centuries) is an edifice of imposing and almost unbelievable dimensions. It is a hundred metres (330 ft.) long, twelve metres (40 ft.) wide and almost nine metres (29.5 ft.) high. A magnificent wide stairway leads up to the palace façade. Eleven columnar doorways and two rectangular openings give access to twenty vaulted rooms. The palace is built on a raised platform 13 m (43 ft.) high overlooking a vast artificial esplanade. Such man-made "acropolises" made it possible to place buildings above surrounding treetops, high enough to avoid humidity during the rainy season and catch the slightest breeze during tropical heat waves.

The terrace which supports the Palace of the Governors at Uxmal is 180 m (590 ft.) from front to back, 154 m (505 ft.) from side to side and 12 m (40 ft.) from top to bottom. This enormous earth platform includes a sum total of 300,000 cubic metres (392,400 cubic yards) of building materials. How could such colossal earthworks be erected in cities where there were neither cranes nor wheeled vehicles?

Burdens were carried by human porters. One can imagine Maya building sites swarming with workers carrying baskets on their heads and hods on their backs. One man could carry about 50 kg (110 lbs.) at each trip. If the building site was only 2 km (1.2 mi.) from the quarry, he could make the round trip in an hour. A full-time worker could transport 500 kg (1100 lbs.) daily. Since at least two thousand workers were probably set to this task, they transported all in all 1000 tons of building materials daily. Supposing there were two hundred working days in a year, the construction of the esplanade supporting the Palace of the Governors would have taken three years. Such an output could have been possible only in a highly organized society. It indeed seems extremely probable that the Maya, like most agrarian theocracies, had a rigorously hierarchic social structure.

Prefabrication and Mass Production

The Palace of the Governors is composed of a central building and two wings separated by slightly concave corbeled arches typical of lowland Maya architecture. An exuberant geometric frieze crowns the edifice. On this decorative band Greek key-patterns forming latticework relief alternate with strange mask motifs. Taken as a whole, the frieze seems to be composed of a series of wavy lines resembling mythological sky-serpents. The stylized mask motifs are repeated on the corners of the building.

The haunting features of these masks, constantly repeated and transformed, entirely cover the façades of later Maya monuments. They are the result of a process of stylization initiated at the dawn of high Maya civilization in Petén, in particular at Uaxactún in the second century B.C. Some masks portray Chac, the rain-god. Others represent Itzamná, head of the Maya pantheon, god of creation.

Repetition and geometric abstraction are the two main guiding principles governing the decorative friezes which cover the façades of Puuc

This wide stairway flanked by two low buildings leads to the northern palace of the Nunnery Quadrangle. The richly decorated frieze including motifs resembling primitive Maya huts was originally crowned by a series of crests made up of superimposed Chac-masks. Eleven doors open on to the inner court.

Above:
Eastern palace of the Nunnery Quadrangle at Uxmal dating from A.D. 909.

monuments. Lowland Maya art is indeed a spectacular example of mass production. The decorative band encircling the Palace of the Governors at Uxmal covers an area of 700 sqaure metres (840 square yards). The frieze includes about 150 masks portraying Chac. That means 300 eyes, 300 horns, 300 big curved fangs, 300 ears each of which is composed of two identical segments with an empty space in between, i.e. 600 identical segments. The masks are joined in a latticework stone mosaic. The background alone includes more than 10,000 identical segments.

One should not forget that all these segments had to be fitted together with mathematical precision; they were not only meant as decoration. Stone mosaics also served as facings (the lower sections of the façades were faced in plain limestone veneer) and casing for concrete work. All play had to be eliminated. If the error had exceeded one centimetre per segment, it would have been impossible to assemble the frieze.

The workshops of Maya stone-cutters and sculptors were actually gigantic factories where prefabricated parts were mass produced. The great number of identical segments which go to make up Puuc decorative friezes leads us to believe that Maya craftsmen had developed a system similar to the· modern assembly-line.

No other method can explain the admirable finished product as we see it today at Uxmal. Is it not astounding to discover the existence of procedures foretelling modern industrial techniques such as prefabrication, assembly-line production and division of labour, in an essentially neolithic culture? The sociological consequences are, needless to say, of

View of the façade of the western building of the Nunnery Quadrangle from a room in the northern palace.

Below:
Detail of a Chac-mask. The rain-god is characterized by a long pendulous nose.

Detail of the frieze decorating the western palace. We can see a human head peeping from the open-fanged mouth of the Feathered Serpent, Kukulcán. This decorative band was added by the Toltecs during the Postclassic period.

great importance: this kind of observation teaches us more about the hierarchic structure of Maya society than many learned treatises.

The Nunnery Quadrangle at Uxmal is a group of four freestanding palaces about a large court. This complex rises up at the foot of the massive Pyramid of the Magician which offsets the patio. It was originally inhabited by Maya priests. The Nunnery Quadrangle is an excellent example of Maya site planning characterized by a very clever utilization of space and distribution of masses. Monumental stairways lead up to the triumphal arch adorning the façade of the southern palace. When one enters the large court, one is surprised to find that the enclosed area marked off by the four palaces comprises serveral differrent levels. The buildings on either side are slightly raised on wide tiers, while on the north the largest palace towers above a long flight of stairs flanked by two low buildings. Dimensions are grandiose; the court is 80 m (260 ft.) long and 65 m (210 ft.) wide.

Lavish decoration by no means diminishes the marvellous simplicity of the Nunnery Quadrangle. This palace complex with its open angles and terraced arrangement may be considered as the masterpiece of lowland Maya architecture. The latest recorded Initial Series date was moreover discovered in the Nunnery Quadrangle at Uxmal: A.D. 909.

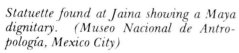

Statuette found at Jaina showing a Maya dignitary. (Museo Nacional de Antropología, Mexico City)

Like the Romans, the lowland Maya raised monuments ressembling triumphal arches. The famous archway at Labná dating from the eighth or ninth century leads to a rectangular court surrounded by palaces. The frieze displays motifs resembling Maya huts with thatched roofs.

24

Palace at the site of Xtampak, buried under rank overgrowth. The chief Maya ceremonial centres have now been freed from their leafy prison and patiently restored by archaeologists.

Detail of the Chac-masks covering the entire façade of the palace at Kabah, near Uxmal, known as the Codz-Poop, or Palace of the Masks. More than 250 identical mass produced sculptured segments are placed side by side and tier upon tier.

Below right:

Many Maya villages still display traditional huts identical to those shown in friezes decorating pre-Columbian palaces. The thatched roof covers an oblong area enclosed by semicircular adobe walls. The hut is windowless and there is only one doorway in the front wall. The adobe walls provide excellent heat insulation. The dark narrow rooms in Maya palaces were stone copies of such primitive huts.

Chichén Itzá : the Maya-Toltec Renaissance

Postclassic votive stone axe in the shape of a skull. Maya thought and religion underwent far-reaching transformations after the Toltec invasion. These "hachas" were probably used in religious ceremonies involving human sacrifice. (Private collection)

In the tenth century of the Christian era a great revolution in Maya civilization took place at Chichén Itzá in northeastern Yucatán. This upheaval was caused by the invasion of the Toltec tribe migrating from their legendary capital of Tollán (Tula) in the highlands of central Mexico. The result was an extraordinary cultural revival which checked for a time the decline of this great pre-Columbian civilization.

Even before these events took place, Chichén Itzá was already an important Yucatecan religious and political centre. In the southern part of the city monuments such as the Nunnery, Iglesia (a small shrine) and the famous Caracol ("snail") observatory — so named on account of the spiral staircase which leads to the summit of the cylindrical tower — exhibit a purely classic influence. Decoration is more lavish than at Uxmal and appears at times almost baroque. Nonetheless, most of these edifices built from the seventh to the tenth century A.D. principally recall the Puuc style.

In actual fact, each and every Maya city elaborated its own particular mode of artistic expression, original aesthetic standards and an unmistakable regional style. Such local variants lead us to believe that the Maya empire was not a unified centralized system but a confederation of more or less independent cities which shared the same gods, the same stock of knowledge and the same cultural heritage. The individual cities — like the Greek city-states — were more or less autonomous in the concert of the Maya world. The diversity of forms and ornamental styles bears witness to this partial independence.

The Astronomical Observatory

The great city of Chichén Itzá was one of the first New World sites excavated by archaeologists. As early as 1906 the Mexican government took steps to preserve the site. In 1923 the Carnegie Institute of Washington D. C. began the task of restoration in cooperation with the Mexican Department of Public Education. Restoration of the various edifices took twenty years. Sylvanus Morley who directed the excavations paid special attention to the Caracol observatory.

The Caracol (or "snail") observatory at Chichén Itzá was built in the late ninth or early tenth century, a short time before the decline of Classic period Maya civilization. The edifice is a veritable stroke of skill which well proves the virtuosity of Maya architects. The cylindrical tower, 12 m (40 ft.) in diameter, rises up on a rectangular platform which covers an area of 500 square metres (600 square yards) and is in turn supported by a vast terrace covering an area of 3500 square metres (4200 square yards). The lower terrace underwent several alterations. The tower itself comprises two concentric rings and a central core. The two

26

ring chambers thus obtained are vaulted in accordance with a classic technique of Maya architecture, here applied for the first and last time to a circular structure completely different from primitive huts. A spiral staircase contrived within the central core gives access to the upper chamber. Loopholes for sighting were pierced in the walls of this room 24 m (79 ft.) above the ground.

Inscriptions and Scientific Achievements

This complex of rings and circular vaults was built with a purpose. The staggered doors and staircases, multiple terraces and upper chamber complete with loopholes were constructed with regard mainly to a function rather than to aesthetic considerations. Morley proved that the Caracol tower was meant to be an astronomical abservatory. The three remaining loopholes in the half-ruined upper chamber make it possible to find geographic east and south and ascertain the point on the horizon where the sun rises at the spring equinox. Astronomers could

also establish the position of the setting moon at its northernmost and southernmost points.

In order to understand the importance of the Caracol observatory for Maya civilization, we must tackle the problem of hieroglyphic inscriptions and mathematical, astronomical and scientific acquisitions. Calendrical concepts are of particular importance for all pre-Columbian civilizations but especially for the Maya who worshipped time.

Maya writing has been preserved on stone stelae, molded-stucco relief decoration, wooden doors, ceramic vessels and jade ornaments, to say nothing of the pre-Conquest codices written on bark paper the front and

Postclassic polychrome clay head found at Mayapán. Tlaloc, the rain-god, is depicted with fangs, a head-band and ear ornaments. Artists have given him a dreadful yet serene expression symbolizing gentle spring showers as well as devastating storms. (Museo Nacional de Antropología, Mexico City)

rear surfaces of which were given a smooth white coating of lime. Maya hieroglyphic writing comprised from 800 to 1,000 symbols, or glyph elements. At the present time only 200 glyphs have been deciphered by specialists. Anglo-Saxon scholars have attempted to clarify the problem set by Maya inscriptions. Their basic source of information is the sixteenth century work of the Fransiscan Diego de Landa, *Relación de las Cosas de Yucatán*. Morley, Gann and Thompson are among those who have made the greatest contributions to deciphering mathematical and astronomical texts. Their studies have enabled us to read numbers and names of days, months and deities (many gods of the Maya codices symbolize days and numbers). However it is still difficult to form an accurate idea of the symbols used by the Maya to represent their common vocabulary. The glyphs deciphered are unquestionably

Southern part of Chichén Itzá with its monuments recalling the Puuc style. To the right, the façade of the Iglesia. In the background, the terraces supporting the cylindrical tower known as the Caracol ("snail") observatory on account of its spiral staircase.

Above:
At the corner of the small structure known as the Iglesia (Church) at Chichén Itzá, an effigy of Chac with his long pendulous nose recalling a tapir's proboscis.

ideographic. But we are entitled to suppose that at least some of the other symbols had phonetic value. If all the glyphs were ideographic, it would have been impossible to note the several thousand words which go to make up even the most primitive language. We are therefore obliged to admit that some Maya hieroglyphics were used for representing sounds and not ideas. The same phenomenon can moreover be remarked in ancient Egypt and Babylonia.

As we have already said, the symbols representing numbers have now been deciphered. This achievement was a great victory for both archaeologists and historians: knowledge of the meaning of these glyphs is indeed essential if we wish to understand Maya astronomy, chronology and calendrical concepts. We can now read dates recorded on stelae and stairways in the ancient ceremonial centres of Petén and Chiapas. Luckily for historians, the Maya customarily recorded dates on all important monuments.

Although Landa was the first scholar who took an interest in Maya civilization, he committed almost all their books to the flames when he became bishop at Mérida in 1572. Nonetheless, his accounts have enabled us to understand the astoundingly intricate mathematics elaborated by Maya priests. For numerical recording, the Maya used a vigesimal system of position numerals. Whereas our decimal system is based on multiples of 10, the Maya system was based on multiples of 20.

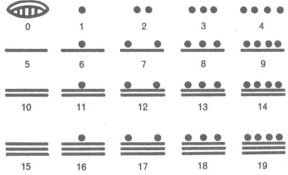

The Sacred Cenote at Chichén Itzá, a natural water hole formed by the collapse of the limestone surface crust. It is 50 m (164 ft.) in diameter; its water level is 20 m (66 ft.) below ground level, with a water depth of 13 m (43 ft.). After the Toltec invasion it was used for ceremonial rites connected with Tlaloc, the rain-god. In order to gain the good will of the god, priests threw young men into the well where they drowned. Archaeologists have retrieved offerings from its depths, including gold and jade ornaments.

Above:
Maya numbers from 1 to 19.

Our first position includes the number 1 to 9; in the second position each unit has the value of 10, in third position the value of 100, etc. Maya first position included the numbers 1 to 19; in the second position each unit had the value of 20, in the third position the value of 400, etc. Such a system of position numerals would have been impossible without the concept of zero. Zero was represented by a stylized clam shell. A dot denoted 1 and a horizontal bar 5. Distinct symbols represented the numbers 1 to 19. The Maya wrote numbers from bottom to top. For example, three superposed bars topped by two dots represented the number 17. The vigesima system enabled Maya mathematicians to juggle with enormous numbers. In the decimal system, a six-figure number has a value between 100,000 and 999,999. In the vigesimal system the value of the same number can go from 160,000 to 3,199,999.

Maya numerical recording was most ingenious, much more so than the Greek or Roman systems. This neolithic civilization invented the concept of zero — fundamental for the birth of modern science.

Astronomy and Calendrical Concepts

The Maya vigesimal system has only one exception: concerning the computation of the days. They go from the first to the second column at 18 instead of 20. This exception is the result of the solar year calcula-

tion. For, the calendar counts 18 months of 20 days with 5 additional days. The notation, when concerning the computation changes the column at 360, 7,200, 144,000, 2,880,000 and so on.

Knowledge of mathematics combined with astronomical studies produced a highly accurate calendar. For all agrarian civilizations, prosperity depends on the ability to predict changing seasons, in particular the beginning of the rainy season when crops were sown and reaped. No calendar can exist without some knowledge of astronomy; Maya time cycles were derived from the movements of celestial bodies.

The Maya calendar is extremely complicated. It comprises three time cycles : a solar calendar of 365 days (known as the Vague Year), a ritual calendar of 260 days, and an astronomical calendar of 584 days based on the synodical revolution of the planet Venus. Eight solar years are equal to five Venus cycles. The solar year (composed of 18 months of 20 days each, with a period of 5 days added at the end) was also used to calculate the "katun", a period of 20 Vague Years, or 7,200 days (the 5 extra days were not counted). The "katun" was denoted by means of a special glyph. Long Count calendrical computations were based on increasing multiples of 20. The "kinchiltun", or great-great-great cycle, was a period of 3,200,000 tuns, or solar years of 360 days each, i.e. 1,152,000,000 days !

The Calendar Round was computed by the permutation of the solar calendar with the 260-day ritual calendar. This special cycle was 18,980 days long. The same date recurred every 52 years.

Maya Long Count or Initial Series dates were computed from a mythical starting point corresponding to 3113 B.C. No archaeological vestiges dating from this period have been found in the New World.

Facing page :
Façade of the Nunnery at Chichén Itzá. In the foreground, a corner of the Iglesia. These two structures dating from the eighth or ninth century display Toltec influence.

During the Postclassic Toltec period at Chichén Itzá, the art style was marked by austerity and geometric stylization. Feathered serpent motifs portraying the god Quetzalcóatl (known as Kukulcán in the Yucatán peininsula) are a diagnostic feature of Postclassic architecture. Feathered serpents are placed on either side of the stairways, as if to defend the sanctuaries. In the foreground, the Stairway leading to the Platform of the Eagles. In the background, the Temple of the Jaguars adjacent to the great ball court.

Remarkable Statistical Computations

Maya priests applied their knowledge of mathematics to astronomy by means of what we would now call statistical methods. Astronomical observations were frequently repeated over a long period of time. The arithmetic mean gave remarkably accurate measurements, though pre-Columbian astronomers had no telescopes or other optical instruments.

According to the Dresden Codex, the lunar calendar was established on the basis of the observation of 405 lunations (which represent observations over a thirty-three year period), a period estimated at 11,960 days. According to modern astronomers, the length of this period is 11,959.888 days. The difference between the two estimations is approximately one day every 380 years. The margin of error is less than 4 minutes per year, i.e. 17 seconds per lunation. For a people who possessed absolutely no time-measuring instruments, a margin of error of less than 20 seconds a month is almost unbelievable.

The Dresden Codex is mainly concerned with study of the Venus cycle. Venus, the brightest planet in the firmament, can be seen before sunset and keeps shining after sunrise. Maya computation of the length of the synodical revolution of the planet Venus was astoundingly accurate. In order to obtain a satisfactory estimation, observations were repeated over a period of 384 years. According to Maya astronomers, the length of the Venus cycle was 584 days. The revolution of the planet Venus is now estimated at 583.92 days. The Maya margin of error was equal to one hour and twelve minutes per year.

Maya astronomers measured only the apparent movement of celestial bodies, as if the earth were the centre of the universe. What methods did they use besides mathematical computations? We have already mentioned sighting angles: heliacal rising and setting with respect to the ecliptic which enabled them to establish the dates of solstices and equinoxes. Estimated angles of inclination must also have been taken into account: for example the elevation of Venus above the horizon at sunrise on June 21st (summer solstice). Such combinations made it possible for the Maya to tell time without clocks!

The Toltec Invasion

In the tenth century, settled Mexican civilizations were subjugated by waves of invaders who swept down from the north. The same phenomenon had occurred five hundred years before after the fall of Teotihuacán, the great highland capital. The town of Tula, north of Mexico City, was seized by nomadic warriors who put the entire population to flight. After the fall of Tula, many Toltec refugees were received among the Itzá, an aggressive seafaring people who first invaded the Yucatán from the east in A.D. 918. Driven out of the highlands, the former inhabitants of Tula migrated to Cholula, the Tabasco-Campeche Gulf Coast and parts of Central America. Their first stop was El Tajín, a Totonac city near the Gulf Coast. Leaving El Tajín, the Toltecs and Itzá moved on towards northeastern Yucatán. Maya civilization was already on the wane. The invaders encountered but little resistance.

A prophetic text, the "Book of Chilam Balam", written by Yucatecan Maya in European script shortly after the Spanish Conquest, recounts the odyssey of the Itzá in search of a new fatherland and their conquest of Uucilabnal, an ancient Maya city, renamed Chichén Itzá (A.D. 987). They had left their homeland a thousand kilometres behind them...

A genuine renaissance took place in northern Yucatán under the influence of the newcomers. This cultural revival continued from the tenth through the twelfth century. Its geographic scope was extremely limited. The new art style produced by the coalescence of Maya and Toltec traditions flourished mainly at Chichén Itsá and Mayapán. The newcomers assimilated the culture of their predecessors. The result was

View of the ball court from the summit of the Castillo. One can distinguish the south end of the playing area with its high facing walls. To the right, a low-relief showing a Maya dignitary.

Skull carved in the round decorating a corner of the Tzompantli.

Above:
Detail of the carved representations of severed heads decorating the Tzompantli at Chichén Itzá. The heads of sacrificial victims were skewered to this 60 m (197 ft.) long skull rack.

an art style completely different from the creations of the Maya Classic period. Unlike the exuberant art of the Classic period, Postclassic Toltec art is grandiose, tragic, awe-inspiring. This change reflects the transformation undergone by Maya thought and religion after the invasion. The Itzá brought with them a new deity worshiped throughout Central America: Quetzalcóatl (Kukulcán). The new religion was centred upon human sacrifice.

During the Maya Classic period, divine worship also called for sacrifices and libations: burnt copal, raw or cooked food, animal or human blood. In auto-sacrifice Maya ascetics pierced their tongues or the lobes of their ears with the sting of a stingray and offered up their blood to the gods. Nonetheless, human sacrifice by cardiotomy was not unknown. Low-reliefs at Piedras Negras and murals discovered at Bonampak in 1946 bear witness to the existence of human sacrifice during the Classic period. It seems however that these sacrifices were originally quite infrequent. After the Toltec invasion, human sacrifices increased in number. The victims were mainly captives. Toltec religious ceremonies foretell Aztec ritual massacres. At Chichén Itzá human victims were offered up to the gods even before the invasion. They were thrown into the Sacred Cenote, or Well of Sacrifice, where they drowned...

Maya-Toltec Architecture

The last distinct art style produced by the Maya world flourished at the sacred city of Chichén Itzá. We would however be mistaken in believing it to be wholly derived from native Yucatecan traditions. The Postclassic style was the result of a symbiosis in which Maya techniques were combined with the art of the Toltec and Itzá invaders. Architecture underwent far reaching transformations. The site of Chichén Itzá has more in common with Tula than with Classic Maya ceremonial centres. The layout of the Temple of the Warriors at Chichén Itzá is borrowed from the Atlantean Pyramid (or Pyramid of Tlahuizcalpantecuhtli, god of the Morning Star, our planet Venus) at Tula. We see at both sites the same entrance colonnade, monumental stairway, storeyed pyramid, serpent-columns and decorative friezes depicting heart-devouring eagles and jaguars. In short, everything is alike. The one and only distinguishing feature is the Maya corbeled arch and vault. The Itzá turned this concept to the best account in the construction of their hypostyle halls.

The hypostyle hall in the Temple of the Warriors combines the Maya vault — unknown in the rest of pre-Columbian Mexico and Central

View from the Tzompantli, or Skull Rack, at Chichén Itzá. In the background, the Platform of the Eagles.

The Platform of the Eagles at Chichén Itzá exhibits visible Toltec influence. Four stairways lead up to the square platform. The monument is decorated with narrative relief panels showing feathered serpent motifs and heart-devouring eagles and jaguars.

View of the Castillo at Chichén Itzá from the raised viewing platforms lining the ball court and attached Temple of the Jaguars.

Toltec warrior at Chichén Itzá wearing a lavish feather headdress, an emblematic jaguar-shaped breastplate and ear ornaments bearing the effigy of the sun-god.

America — with columns and pillars. The famous Hall of a Thousand Columns is composed of dozens of such supports. Long parallel bays run back from the open façade, perpendicularly to the axis of penetration. The result hardly seems possible. The massive walls which formerly supported heavy Maya concrete vaults have been replaced by some fifty columns connected by horizontal beams. This daring technique made it possible to create a roofed enclosure originally covering an area of over 750 square metres (900 square yards).

The difference in size is not merely quantitative; it is the result of an attempt to meet new and different needs. The weakness of the Maya corbeled arch required massive walls and supports. The narrow dark rooms characteristic of Classic period Maya architecture were perfect for dignitaries who shut themselves up in their narrow individualism and scholars immersed in meditation. Toltec warriors, members of the orders of Eagles and Jaguars, needed spacious places of assembly for the performance of their sanguinary rites and mass displays of courage.

The Castillo, the most prominent pyramid at Chichén Itzá, also dates back to the tenth or eleventh century. It is a leveled square pyramid composed of a series of nine rising tiers of decreasing dimensions. Four stairways, one on each side, lead up to the temple. The structure is 33 m (110 ft.) high. Each side is 55 m (180 ft.) long. Each stairway has 91 steps, i.e. 364 all in all plus yet one more at the entrance to the temple to make a total of 365 equal to the number of days in the solar year. At the foot of the stairways monumental "feathered serpent" motifs represent the god Kukulcán.

Two sides of this imposing structure have been damaged by vegetation. The other two are extremely well preserved. When archaeologists began restoring the Castillo, they ascertained that the pyramid was built on top of an earlier similar structure. Such superimpositions are so frequent in the pre-Columbian world that archaeologists usually make borings to establish the history of the monuments they restore. The

View of the Temple of the Warriors at Chichén Itzá from the Castillo. This pyramid dating back to the eleventh century displays nine rising tiers and four axial stairways. The structure is 55 m (180 ft.) on a side and 30 m (98 ft.) high. Feathered serpents guard the entrance to the temple.

restorers of the Castillo at Chichén Itzá were amazed at discovering beneath the temple at the summit of the pyramid another similar temple buried in the heart of the edifice. This lower temple was perfectly intact. Inside the chamber where no man had set foot for almost a thousand years, archaeologists found a sanctuary in the same condition in which priests had left it after the last ceremony. The entrance housed a Chacmool (life-sized statue of a god or man lying on his back with flexed legs, hands holding a flat receptacle to receive offerings). The throne of the red jaguar behind the Chacmool was decorated with 73 jade inlays simulating the sacred animal's spotted coat.

The Downfall of Maya Civilization

The economy, as in all agrarian societies, was based on the output of the peasant class. The peasants supported the entire population. Excess production made it possible to stock provisions for future needs and ensured subsistence to craftsmen and noblemen. The craftsmen most often worked for the benefit of the members of the ruling caste and the gods they served. This system resulted in concentration of power in the hands of a religious oligarchy. The increasing demands of the ruling caste called for more and more peasant labour. An outside impulse alone could shake the prodigious Maya social structure and bring about the liberation of the rural class. Destabilization followed the great migrations which swept over Yucatán after barbaric tribes invaded Central Meza.

When the revolt finally broke out, it proved irrepressible. It spread over the country like an epidemic. In three generations it had entirely covered the central region: work ceased everywhere, stelae were left unfinished, writing was no longer used and Initial Series dates were not recorded. The last inscriptions enable us to follow the victorious advance of the revolted peasants: Palenque, 782; Copán, 801; Tikal, 869; Uxmal, 909. The Toltecs took Chichén Itzá 987.

Facing page:
Temple of the Warriors at Chichén Itzá. A Chacmool is centred in front of two serpent columns marking the entrance to the sanctuary.

Facing page, below:
Low-relief showing a Maya-Toltec warrior armed with a lance.

Next pages (40-41):
Temple of the Warriors at Chichén Itzá. The forest of pillars supported Maya corbeled vaults strengthened with timber work. The wooden lintels have rotted away and the roof has collapsed.

Below:
Colonnade at the base of the Temple of the Warriors.

Feathered serpent motif in the Temple of the Warriors.

The first great highland culture of the Classic period had its capital at Teotihuacán, the "City of the Gods", near modern Mexico City. Teotihuacán flourished from the third century B.C. to the fifth century A.D. To the left, the Pyramid of the Moon, recently restored. In the foreground, the Ciudadela. To the right, the enormous Pyramid of the Sun.

The great stairway of the Temple of Quetzalcóatl in the square compound known as the Ciudadela dates back to the first century of the Christian era. The structure is decorated with feathered serpent motifs and masks of Tlaloc, the rain-god.

Teotihuacán and Monte Albán: "Cities of the Gods"

If we leave the lowlands of Yucatán for the high plateaux of Central Meza, we shall discover a pre-Columbian metropolis most unlike Maya ceremonial centres. Far from the dense forest of the lowlands, the city of Teotihuacán which was for several centuries the cultural capital of Mesoamerica rises up at an altitude of 2,300 m (7,550 ft.) at the foot of volcanoes which reach a height of 5,000 m (16,400 ft.). This enormous religious metropolis is situated about 40 kilometres (25 mi.) north of modern Mexico City. It played an important part in the development of pre-Columbian Mesoamerica.

Teotihuacán is a complex of pyramids, esplanades, sacred causeways and majestic palaces. The ceremonial centre proper covers an area of more than 5 square kilometres (2 square miles) in the heart of an urban complex which probably covered an area of 32 square kilometres (12 square miles) when the town was at the height of its glory. This stupen-

Detail of a mask of Tlaloc decorating the stairway of the Temple of Quetzalcóatl at Teotihuacán. The rings about his eyes and volute over his mouth are excellent examples of geometric stylization characteristic of Teotihuacán carvings.

Open-fanged head of the feathered serpent decorating the ramps of the Temple of Quetzalcóatl at Teotihuacán. The silhouette of the Pyramid of the Sun stands out against the mountains on the horizon.

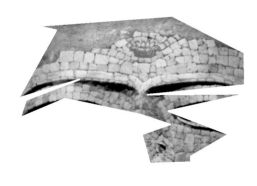

Teotihuacán Classic style carved stone face mask: serpentine inlaid with shell, turquoise and obsidian.

Above:
Monolithic statue of the water-goddess found at the site of Teotihuacán. (Museo Nacional de Antropología, Mexico City)

Above right:
Quetzalpapalotl Palace at Teotihuacán, built about A.D. 250. Porticoes with carved pillars run along the sides of the court.

One of the polychrome murals decorating most of the inner walls of the temples and palaces at Teotihuacán: mythological felines.

dous cultural complex is the largest and most imposing creation of pre-Columbian town-planners. We are surprised by the monumental dimensions, clever utilization of space and rigorous execution of the overall plan.

This ancient capital fell in ruins long before the arrival of the conquistadores. The Aztecs regarded it as a mythical site founded by the gods themselves. This explains why they named these grandiose ruins the "City of the Gods". They knew nothing about the men who had erected these colossal monuments which they sincerely revered.

A Prodigious Ceremonial Centre

The Pyramid of the Sun, the most prominent monument of the sacred city of Teotihuacán, is one of the largest structures in Mesoamerica. Its builders must have had a highly developed civilization. The pyramid is 225 m (740 ft.) long and 222 m (730 ft.) wide at its base and covers an area of 50,000 square metres (59,800 square yards). It is built in five terraces to a temple platform 63 m (207 ft.) above the valley floor. The total volume of the edifice exceeds one million cubic metres, i.e. more than two million tons of building materials.

The next most important edifice at Teotihuacán is the Pyramid of the

Moon. It is 150 m (492 ft.) long and 140 m (460 ft.) wide at its base and covers an area of about 20,000 square metres (24,000 square yards), i.e. two hectares (5 acres). It reaches a height of 42 m (140 ft.) and occupies a volume of nearly 300,000 cubic metres (390,000 cu. yards).

In addition to these two colossal pyramids, the civic-religious centre of Teotihuacán includes a monumental causeway known as the Avenue of the Dead though it had nothing to do with funeral ceremonies. Clusters of buildings are aligned along the avenue which is more than 2 km (1.2 mi.) long. At the north end of the avenue, the Pyramid of the Moon overlooks a large rectangular plaza (known as the Court of the Moon) surrounded by terraced platforms. The Avenue of the Dead runs along the western side of the Pyramid of the Sun and leads to a vast square compound known as the Ciudadela — the ancient seat of the hierarchy — which contains the Temple of Quetzalcóatl, the omnipresent Feathered Serpent.

Age of the City of Teotihuacán

When was this grandiose city (the earliest true urban complex in Middle America) erected? Who built these fantastic black basalt artificial mountains ressembling the volcanoes that rise up on the horizon?

View of the Great Plaza at Monte Albán from the North Platform: an enormous religious centre composed of quadrangular plazas surrounded by pyramids and stairways. The Zapotec capital reached the height of its power about A.D. 400–700 but the site itself was inhabited as far back as the seventh century B.C. Like a balcony overlooking surrounding valleys, the city of the priest-kings of central Mexico seems to be hung half way between heaven and earth.

Facing page, above:

Funerary urn found in a tomb at Monte Albán: intricate ornamentation represents the deities of the Zapotec pantheon with all their attributes. (Museo Nacional de Antropología, Mexico City)

Facing page, below:

"System M" pyramid at Monte Albán. A monumental stairway leads to the raised platform supporting a badly destroyed temple. To the far right, the low-relief sculptures of the "Danzantes".

The true age of Teotihuacán has given rise to much controversy among specialists. After the diggings undertaken in 1962 by Ignacio Bernal, then director of the National Museum at Mexico City, analysis of carbon 14 found in the rafters of a palace excavated near the Court of the Moon has made it possible to date these stupendous monuments.

These new facts seem to prove that the site of Teotihuacán is some 250 years older than it was formerly believed. The foundation of Teotihuacán probably dates back to the fifth century B.C. The Pyramid of the Sun was erected in the third century B.C. The Avenue of the Dead and the Pyramid of the Moon date back to the second century B.C. The Ciudadela and the Temple of Quetzalcóatl were built at the dawn of the Christian era.

The famous palace in the rafters of which carbon 14 was found — the so-called Quetzalpapalotl Palace — was built about A.D. 250. Two hundred years later invaders swooped down from the north and systematically destroyed the palaces and ceremonial centre. From 450 to 650 the city survived somehow or other but in the seventh century repeated invasions put the inhabitants to flight and the site was abandoned.

An Architectural Innovation: the Talud-Tablero

One sole principle governs the arrangement of the rectilinear vistas and well defined volumes of Teotihuacán, a constant feature the repetition of which creates a kind of rhythmic obsession. Indeed, all the structures that go to make up this complex of espalanades, platforms, pyramids and courts exhibit the same classic architectural feature, the same standard of proportion and the same stereotyped outline. This constant feature is not a mere decorative motif but a genuine building technique peculiar to Teotihuacán architecture. The feature in question is a rectangular panel which Mexican archaeologists call a "tablero".

The panel's frame encloses a recessed surface often decorated with painted or sculptured motifs.

These panels were cantilevered over a sloping wall, or "talud". The feature was repeated on the receding walls of stepped temple pyramids. The friability of lime mortar and other building materials used by the pre-Columbians rendered the construction of high sustaining walls impossible. Architects obliged to give up the idea of perpendicular retaining walls strengthened with masonry, resorted to a system of rising tiers. The talud-tablero architectural feature enabled them moreover to avoid blurred outlines often characteristic of volumes defined by oblique lines and inclined planes. The tablero was superimposed at regular intervals over a larger sloping talud so as to create a chiaroscuro effect and maximize the play of light and shadow in the strong sun of the tropics.

Two rule governed the use of panels at Teotihuacán. The first and most important one was an orthogonal layout. The various elements were arranged according to an overall plan so as to form right angles. The edifices were aligned along a north-south axis borrowed from the Olmec. Symmetry, the second guiding principle, was actually a mere corollary of this orthogonal layout. The construction of each building or group of buildings was bound by strict axial symmetry. Stairways also played an important part in the overall appearance of the site.

Pyramid Structure

The two great pyramids were both built according to the same principle : the three lower tiers (with trapezoidal sides) are separated from the fourth upper tier by a perpendicular ressaut. The upper platform originally supported a temple. Only the foundations of the walls now remain. Along with stone and terra-cotta models unearthed at the site

View of the Great Plaza at Monte Albán from the South Platform. In the foreground, the observatory built in the shape of a ship's prow.

Below:
I-shaped ball court a Monte Albán. The parallel facing walls were originally coated with stucco and polychromed.

Detail of a scapulary tablet characteristic of Zapotec architecture. The decorative panel, or tablero, was superimposed over a sloping wall..

by archaeologists, they make it possible for us to imagine what the temple probably looked like. The temple contained only one room. Priests alone were allowed to enter.

The monumental stairway that leads to the temple crowning the Pyramid of the Sun begins as two distinct flights of stairs, one on each side of the first tier which juts out on the pyramid's western façade. These two flights meet at the top of the first tier, divide at the base of the third tier and meet once again at the base of the perpendicular ressaut.

The Pyramid of the Sun may well have been devoted to sun-worship. Its orientation is based on the point on the horizon at which the sun sets on June 21st. The two distinct stairways could be intended to symbolize days getting longer and shorter. Depending on the dates of the various ceremonies, priests may have gone up the southern stairs and come down the northern one or vice versa.

Archaeologists who made borings in 1960 discovered an earlier structure buried in the heart of the pyramid. These borings also furnished us with information about the mode of construction. The pyramid has a mud core made up of several densely packed horizontal layers. In order to protect this friable material from rain, architects capped it with a shell of volcanic rock bonded with mortar. They also erected perpendicular buttresses on either side of the edifice so as to prevent eventual strain and distortion.

How could a people who had neither cranes nor draught-animals bring together such a tremendous mass of building materials? Teotihuacán architects solved this problem in the same way as the builders of the colossal Maya platforms. The pyramids of Teotihuacán were the result of a collective enterprise. Thousands of peasants were put to work at the building site in the dry season.

Supposing four thousand workers transported 100,000 tons of building materials a year, the construction of the Pyramid of the Sun would have taken over twenty years.

The Ciudadela

The Ciudadela is a tremendous square compound 400 m (1,300 ft.) on a side. The surrounding wall supports terraced platforms placed at regular intervals. Flights of stairs lead up to these platforms. The enclosure itself is a rectangular courtyard 195 m (640 ft.) wide and 235 m (770 ft.) long oriented along a west-east axis. Although the architectural

Three examples of the famous "Danzantes", or dancing figures, at Monte Albán. Primitive hieroglyphics are carved near the figures' mouths. They are the earliest known examples of writing in the New World. These archaic low-reliefs, visibly influenced by the Olmec art style, date back to 650 B.C.

means used are extremely simple, the complex produces an impression of perfection and implacable organization. The Ciudadela with its repeated panels and sculptured decoration and its strict orthogonal layout is a genuine masterpiece of pre-Columbian architecture.

In the eastern part of the courtyard archaeologists have unearthed the pyramid which supported the Temple of Quetzalcóatl. The classic panels facing the six tiers of this stepped pyramid are covered with carved decorations. The principal alternating motifs are masks of the Feathered Serpent god (Quetzalcóatl himself) and Tlaloc, the rain-god. Quetzalcóatl is portrayed as a dragon with protruding eyes and enormous fangs. The dragon's mouth is surrounded by a fiery ruff. The masks of Tlaloc are the result of rigorous geometric stylization. The rain-god is depicted with rings about his eyes and a volute over his mouth. These motifs were originally coated with stucco and polychromed. All in all, not counting the twelve Feathered Serpents lining the main stairway, there were probably 360 such masks, symbolizing the number of days in the solar year.

An identical symbolism characterizes the small shrine placed in the middle of the courtyard. It includes four stairways of 13 steps each, i.e. a total of 52 steps equal to the number of years in the Calendar Round.

The Quetzalpapalotl Palace

The Pyramid of the Moon overlooks a plaza at the north end of the Avenue of the Dead. This plaza, known as the Court of the Moon, also exhibits a central shrine surrounded by a dozen terraced platforms. The Quetzalpapalotl Palace which can now be seen at the west end of the plaza was discovered and restored in 1962. This building was originally the dwellingplace of the high dignitaries of Teotihuacán. The central rectangular patio is surrounded by columnar arcades with flat roofs supported by square stone pillars. On three sides the arcades lead into rooms 8-9 m (26-29 ft.) long and 7 m (23 ft.) wide.

Extraordinary gold pendant found in Tomb 7 at Monte Albán. The upper half depicts two ball players and a Classic I-shaped court. Below we see a solar emblem and a butterfly. This admirable ornament was made by Mixtec goldsmiths in the thirteenth century. (Oaxaca Regional Museum)

Tomb 7 at Monte Albán as it was discovered by Alfonso Caso in 1931. The subterranean chamber, originally a Zapotec tomb, was raised by a Mixtec lord. Enormous stone slabs support a saddleback roof.

Facing page, above:
Human skull inlaid with turquoise mosaic work. The eyes are pierced stone disks. Captives slain by the priests were supposed to attend on the important dead in the nether world. This Mixtec ornament was found at Monte Albán. (Oaxaca Regional Museum)

Magnificent carved pillars adorned with low-reliefs are the most interesting feature of the Quetzalpapalotl Palace. The decoration represents mythological animals, doubtless a cross between the quetzal bird and the butterfly. Quetzalpapalotl can be translated as "precious butterfly". Obsidian and shell inlays enhance the beauty of the low-reliefs which were probably polychromed.

Indeed the whole city, now gray and black on account of the volcanic rock used in its construction, was once gaily coloured. All the buildings in the ceremonial centre were coated with stucco and polychromed.

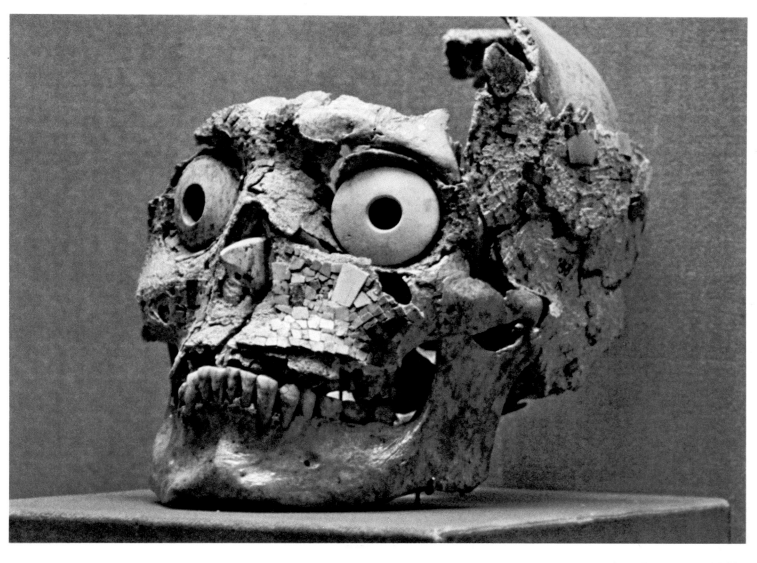

Gold brooch with turquoise inlays and stepped-fret motifs. This Mixtec ornament representing a shield and four javelins was found at the site of Yanhuitlán. (Museo Nacional de Antropología, Mexico City)

Gold bead necklace found in Tomb 7 at Monte Albán. (Oaxaca Regional Museum)

Splendid frescoes covered the banks that run along the walls of the palace chambers. These frescoes, mostly of religious inspiration, depict the Feathered Serpent, the Jaguar-god, the Paradise of Tlaloc, etc.

One of these frescoes, recently discovered, proves the existence of a variant type of the Mesoamerican ball game at Teotihuacán. The mural depicts players armed with sticks resembling base-ball bats. The players are divided into two teams. Goal-posts are placed at both ends of the ball court. One of these goal-posts has been unearthed at Teotihuacán; it ressembles a stone stela crowned with a ring. The ball game was probably played between the two sloping walls that form the boundaries to the Avenue of the Dead in front of the Pyramid of the Sun.

Ruins of the palace complex at Yagul, city-fortress located half way between Monte Albán and Mitla. The site overlooking a fertile plain was occupied as far back as the seventh century B.C. The multiple-court palace built in the tenth century effects the transition between Zapotec and Mextec art.

Monte Albán, the Sacred Acropolis

Leaving the highlands for the valley of Oaxaca, we discover yet another important pre-Columbian civilization developed by the Zapotecs, major builders of Monte Albán. The Zapotec capital is built on a flattened mountaintop in the heart of the state of Oaxaca, 350 km (220 mi.) southeast of Mexico City, in a mountainous region interesected with deep valeys. Three fertile plains meet at the foot of the arid hill of Monte Albán. The pre-Columbian ceremonial centre overlooks the modern city of Oaxaca situated at an altitude of 1,600 m (5,250 ft.).

Thanks to its location on the dividing line between high Mexican civilization and the Maya lowlands, the Zapotec region was a cultural cross-roads where we can remark Olmec and Maya influence as well as features borrowed from Teotihuacán. The mountain itself resembles a religious citadel. The grandiose ruins of Monte Albán ("White Mountain") rise up in serene isolation on the hill-top. This balcony overlooking the valley occupies an almost impregnable strategic position. However the acropolis of Monte Albán was above all a religious centre. Unlike the City of the Gods, nonchalantly spread out in the middle of a vast plain, the Zapotec religious centre is built on a hill-top, a site very poorly suited to the purpose. In order to erect the edifices that cover this 700 m (2,300 ft.) long and 250 m (820 ft.) wide acropolis, Zapotec builders had to level the mountaintop, erect massive restraining walls and contrive terraces before the construction of pyramids, palaces and tombs could begin.

An entire people co-ordinated their efforts and joined forces in reshaping the mountain. The ruins that now cover the hill-top are the result of thousands of years of patient labour and at least five cultural phases. The ceremonial centre as seen today indicates what the city looked like at the zenith of building activity about 500-700 A.D.

In addition to a series of pyramids crowned with temples built in stone and concrete, we can remark an observatory in the shape of a ship's prow. This structure is one of the few exceptions to the north-south site orientation. A sighting tunnel was contrived in the heart of the edifice. Like Teotihuacán, the ceremonial centre of Monte Albán includes dwelling-places reserved for the priests. One of the most remarkable of these habitations is the palace named for the low-relief sculptures of the "Danzantes", or dancing figures adorning the panels. The earliest known examples of writing in Mesoamerica are carved on these low-reliefs. These sculptural carvings, visibly influenced by the Olmec art style, date back to the city's first cultural phase, about 650 B.C.

Examples of writing are scanty. One or two glyphs are timidly placed in front of the figures' mouths as if to represent spoken words. However these glyphs may also indicate the name of the dignitary portrayed. Specialists have not yet succeeded in deciphering these archaic ideograms.

Monumental stairways and talud-tablero building façades recall the architecture of Teotihuacán. Monte Albán is probably the richest and most varied archaeological site in the whole of ancient Mexico. The hill on which the ceremonial centre is built is literally honeycombed with chambered tombs hollowed in the hill-top and covered with large stone slabs. The furniture found in some of these tombs (174 have now been discovered) is magnificent. Ceramic burial urns with high-relief decoration are particularly remarkable. Some of these tombs are covered with frescoes.

Among the works of art discovered in the famous underground tombs of Monte Albán — in particular in Tomb 7, excavated by Caso in 1931 — goldwork is especially worthy of notice. The most amazing pre-Columbian treasure was indeed found in this sepulchre. These masterpieces are now the pride of the Oaxaca Regional Museum. The specialists who examined these beautiful intricate gold ornaments were very surprised to

Mixtec solid gold pendant. The god Xipe Totec is depicted as a priest dressed in the skin of a sacrificial victim. This ornament was found at the site of Coixtlahuaca in the state of Oaxaca. (Museo Nacional de Antropología, Mexico City)

Ball court at Yagul restored by the Mexican archaeologist Ignacio Bernal. The parallel facing walls sloping inwards to the playing area recall the ball court at Monte Albán.

53

discover that the jewels were not Zapotec but Mixtec. A Mixtec lord had been buried at Monte Albán, raising a sepulchre originally intended for a Zapotec prince. This raise leads us to believe that Monte Albán was not entirely abandoned after its decline. The city remained a holy place (the Rome of the peoples of central Mexico) and became a necropolis.

Yagul and Mitla, Mixtec Cities

About A.D. 900 Monte Albán relinquished its dominance over central Mexico and a new people, the Mixtecs, took power in the region. One of the first achievements of the Mixtec federation was the city-fortress of Yagul situated half way between Oaxaca and Mitla. Yagul was recently excavated and restored by Mexican archaeologists.

The palaces are the most remarkable feature of Yagul. The main area is a complex consisting of a palace with six courts. The main rooms open on to the courts. This layout foretells Mitla's freestanding palace structures. The large ball court at Yagul is also very striking. It recalls the I-shaped ball court at Monte Albán; the proportions and parallel facing walls are much the same.

Yagul was occupied as early as the seventh century B.C. It became an important civic centre in the ninth century A.D., somewhat before Mixtec Postclassic expansion which occurred about A.D. 1000. Pre-Columbian architecture reached its zenith at Mitla, the Mixtec capital. The detailed stone mosaic work that decorates palace façades, the vast halls, central courts and inner colonnades are all remarkable architectural achievements. The palaces at Mitla recall the Nunnery Quadrangle at Uxmal, the Classic Maya centre in the Puuc hills of western Yucatán. The site planning and geometric decoration of the façades are indeed quite similar. Mitla architecture seems to have drawn heavily on lowland Maya culture and especially on Uxmal, the capital of the Puuc style which flourished in the ninth century. Mitla like Uxmal with its long horizontal outlines and austere geometric ornamentation is a utopia of contemporaneous architecture.

The central element of the Group of Columns at Mitla is the best example of this mixed style. The plaza, open on the south, is flanked on the east and on the west by two symmetrical palaces. The enormous palace which forms the northern boundary of the square is built on a terrace 50 m (164 ft.) long. The panels facing the edifice are decorated with stone mosaics. The space behind the panels is filled with packed mud which serves as heat insulation. A row of monolithic columns support the flat roof.

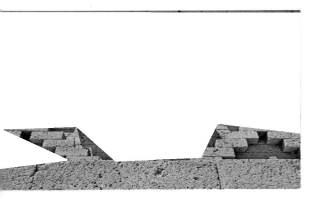

Detail of a geometric stone mosaic decorating the Palace of the Columns at Mitla. This decorative band consists chiefly in variations of the stepped-fret motif.

The columnar hall of the great palace at Mitla opens on to a court. The structure is built of intricately carved stone blocks laid without the use of mortar.

The ornamental motifs which decorate all the façades of this palace are arranged so as to form horizontal panels. The geometric design made up of zigzags, lozenges and Greek key-patterns is slightly different on each panel. The minute details of these decorative stone mosaics are outstanding. The material used is white tuff. Mixtec sculptors were no less skillful than their goldsmiths and jewelers.

The palaces at Mitla had not yet been abandoned when the conquistadores arrived in the New World. Cortés and his companions could see the last Mixtec sovereigns, vassals of the Aztecs, still dwelling in these sumptuous abodes.

View of the southern façade of the Palace of the Columns at Mitla. This architectural masterpiece probably dates from about A.D. 1200. It is remarkably well preserved. The palace is 45 m (148 ft.) long and recalls the monumental dimensions of Puucstyle palaces in western Yucatán.

From the Totonacs to the Peoples of the North

A period of relative unenlightenment followed the downfall of the great Classic period civilizations of Teotihuacán and Monte Albán. The region was shaken by invasions of nomadic warriors until the Aztecs restored order and established a centralized empire.

The Gulf Coast region continued to evolve after the disappearance of the ancient Olmec civilization. The Gulf Coast Classic period flourished from 600 to 1200 at El Tajín, the early capital of the Totonacs. The site of El Tajín is still only partially excavated.

El Tajín was one of the most important regional capitals in ancient Mexico. This Totonac urban centre, situated in the modern state of Veracruz in the torrid lowlands of the Gulf Coast southeast of Mexico City, contains more than a hundred mounds. Some of these mounds rise up on a flat site, others on an acropolis perched on the hills which border the plain on the sea-coast. Twenty years ago the complex was hidden by the dense tropical rain forest.

The central Gulf Coast, homeland of the Totonacs, is famous for its "smiling figure" hollow mold-made figurines. These ceramic sculptures manifest blissful ecstasy. Some archaeologists believe this expression to be the result of hallucinogens given future sacrificial victims. (Private collection)

This low-relief decorating the South Ball Court at El Tajín, early capital of the Totonacs, illustrates the ball game and attendant human sacrifice. The high priest's assistant holds down the victim while the priest prepares to plunge an obsidian knife in his breast. To the left, the god of death. To the right, the ruler, seated on his throne and holding a sceptre, looks on.

56

Pyramid of the Niches, the most prominent monument at El Tajín. Six terraces lead up to the temple. The ramps lining the wide stairway are decorated with stepped-fret motifs. The pyramid, like the South Ball Court, dates from about A.D. 600.

Facing page:

Colima clay figure representing a singing drummer. (Private collection)

Open-fanged head of the feathered serpent worshiped at Xochicalco.

Below:

Detail of a stela at Xochicalco portraying the rain-god.

Pyramid of Quetzalcóatl at Xochicalco. The carved frieze encircling the structure represents a gigantic feathered serpent undulating about seated dignitaries.

The Pyramid of the Niches

The Pyramid of the Niches was the first monument at El Tajín which caught the attention of archaeologists. It was the only edifice that had not been completely invaded by the jungle and hidden under an earthen-shroud. The discovery of the magnificent Totonac capital began with this odd monument. The Pyramid of the Niches was unknown before 1780. Its square base is 35 m (115 ft.) on a side. The pyramid itself is composed of seven rising tiers and reaches a height of 25 m (82 ft.). A large stairway flanked by ramps decorated with the stepped-fret motifs so common in pre-Columbian art leads up the eastern side of the pyramid.

The niches which gave the edifice its name are a diagnostic feature of El Tajín architecture (analogous to talud-tablero facing at Teotihuacán). They roused the curiosity of specialists who first thought they originally contained sculptures. In actual fact, the niches contributed to El Tajín architectural emphasis on chiaroscuro. They also reinforced the sustaining walls and retained the mass of packed clay which made up the structure's core.

Taking into account the niches contrived under the great stairway, the sum total amounts to 365, one for each day in the solar year.

During the Classic period, exchanges took place with Teotihuacán and Monte Albán. The city's main development began about A.D. 600. At its zenith the ceremonial centre covered an area of over 10 square kilometres (4 square miles). Seven ball courts have been found at the site. The most outstanding one is the South Ball Court, adorned with a magnificent low-relief illustrating the ball game and attendant human sacrifice. We know that the ball game was a sacred sport meant to simulate the movement of the sun through the sky. Was the loser offered up as a sacrifice to the gods? This possibility should not be ruled out. There is one stone relief at El Tajín which shows a ball player being sacrificed by the others who are preparing to cut his heart out, overlooked by the death-god.

The site of El Tajín experienced a second major phase of cultural activity characterized by a strong Toltec influence. After the fall of Tula in the tenth century some Toltec refugees settled along the Gulf Coast. The ruins now seen on the acropolis of El Tajín recall the Toltec art style.

Nayarit warrior. (Museo Nacional de Antropología, Mexico City)

Above:
Nayarit figurine: the "thinker". (Private collection)

Above right:
Detail of the face of a Nayarit pottery figure. The ears are pierced. (Museo Nacional de Antropología, Mexico City)

Xochicalco: a Shelter in the Storm

In A.D. 450 nomadic invaders swooping down from the north devastated the ceremonial centre of Teotihuacán. A second invasion about A.D. 650 laid waste to the entire city. The raids of the aggressive northern tribes threw the highlands of central Mexico into a state of upheaval. Only a few isolated sites escaped destruction. One of these havens of refuge was the city of Xochicalco near Cuernavaca where Toltec, Zapotec, Mixtec and Maya influences converged. The city-fortress of Xochicalco, built at an altitude of 1,500 m (4,900 ft.) on an acropolis 130 m (425 ft.) above the surrounding plain, was protected by impregnable fortifications. These defensive works enabled the city's population to withstand the storm which shook the region in the seventh century.

The site of Xochicalco is built on several steep terraced hills joined by rectilinear avenues leading from one level to another. A cultural centre containing several pyramids, two ball courts, dwelling-places and an underground passage overlooks the complex. The main temple is dedicated to Quetzalcóatl. Its four sides are covered with magnificent

Pottery figure in the Nayarit style. The eyes ressemble cowries. (Museo Nacional de Antropología, Mexico City)

Below left:
Nayarit polychrome ceramic figure. (Museo Nacional de Antropología, Mexico City)

Below right:
Detail of a Nayarit figurine wearing a nose-ring. (Museo Nacional de Antropología, Mexico City)

Colima female figure. (Private collection)

low-reliefs depicting a feathered serpent undulating about seated dignitaries. This monument known as the Pyramid of the Feathered Serpent probably supported a square temple 10 m (33 ft.) on a side. Two pairs of columns supported the beams of the roof. Two pillars divided the entrance in three; this concept recalls the Temple of the Warriors at Chichén Itzá and proves Toltec influence at Xochicalco.

Inner Space at Tula

We have already mentioned the city of Tula in connexion with the Maya-Toltec renaissance and the Postclassic phase at El Tajín. One of the main Toltec architectural innovations was the creation of enclosed places of assembly. The Toltecs, a warlike tribe believed to have destroyed the city of Teotihuacán, gradually developed an imposing civilization. They founded a capital north of the City of the Gods. Tula, or Tollán as it is named in some chronicles, was traditionally founded by Ce Ácatl Topiltzin Quetzalcóatl in A.D. 968. The Toltecs made far-reaching innovations in pre-Columbian architecture. They borrowed heavily from Teotihuacán. Orientation and site planning recall the City of the Gods centred round the conspicuous Pyramid of the Sun.

The most prominent edifice at Tula is the Pyramid of Tlahuiz-calpantecuhtli, or Pyramid of the Morning Star, dedicated to the planet Venus. This square pyramid is composed of five rising tiers 35 m (115 ft.) on a side and 10 m (33 ft.) high. A large stairway contrived on the southern façade leads to the upper platform. The Pyramid of the Morning Star at Tula is the prototype of the Temple of the Warriors at Chichén Itzá.

Sculptured architectural innovations included monumental serpent columns and serpent walls (the feathered serpent holds a human head in its openfanged mouth), and processional carved panels of heart-devouring eagles and jaguars. These emblems symbolized Toltec warrior fraternities and were later adopted by the Aztecs.

The temple of Quetzalcóatl has been almost completely destroyed. All

Below left:

Detail of the head of an Atlantean column at Tula. These 4.5 m (15 ft.) high statues are crowned with magnificent feather headdresses. The Toltec art style is austere and imposing.

Pyramid of Tlahuizcalpantecuhtli, god of the morning star, at Tula. The Toltec capital was founded in 856 in the highlands north of Teotihuacán.

that now remains are the monumental sculptured roof-supports. These 4.5 m (15 ft.) high statues carved in the round resemble atlantes or caryatids. They depict warriors wearing feather head-dresses and butterfly-shaped breastplates. Two enormous cylindrical serpent columns rise up in front of the entrance. The serpent's open-fanged head serves as a base and its tail-rattles are the roof support. This Toltec inspired architectural support can also be seen at Chichén Itzá.

Toltec temples at Tula recall the Temple of Quetzalcóatl at Xochicalco. Toltec architecture added, however, colonnaded edifices several ranks deep. The arrival of the northern invaders seems to have greatly modified the pre-Columbian socio-religious system. During the Postclassic period, temples were built to meet the needs of a military oligarchy. The vast inner spaces and hypostyle halls created by Toltec architects were intended as places of assembly for the members of the warrior fraternities.

The monolithic basalt Atlantean supports on the platform of the pyramid of the morning star at Tula wear wide belts and butterfly-shaped breastplates. The fourth statue to the left is a copy; the original can now be seen at the Museo Nacional de Antropología at Mexico City. These massive columns supported the roof of the temple destroyed by Chichimec invaders in 1168.

The Peoples of the North and their Pottery

Architecture is the best clue to guide us through the labyrinth of pre-Columbian civilization. On the Pacific coast of northwestern Mexico monuments are however very scarce. The peoples who inhabited these regions created splendid ceramic figural sculptures.

Colima, Nayarit and Jalisco are the three most prominent western Mexico art styles. Their ceramic figures are quite natural and unconstrained. Colima, Nayarit and Jalisco sculptures recall the pottery peculiar to Pacific coastal Peru (Moche creations in particular). Ceramics come mostly from shaft tombs. Specialists believe these works of art date back to about A.D. 300–900.

Facing page, below right:
Polychrome low-reliefs displaying skull motifs decorate the coatepantli, or serpent wall, at Tula.

The Aztec Empire

Although the Aztecs were late comers in pre-Columbian history, their tumultuous rise to power marked the zenith of Postclassic civilization in pre-Conquest Mexico. Unlike Maya and Zapotec civilization or Classic period Teotihuacán, the Aztec empire was the result of unceasing wars. The Aztec people was composed of seven tribes: the Acolhua, Chalca, Mexica, Tepaneca, Tlalhuica, Tlaxcalteca and Xochimilca. The Aztec empire grew out of the aggressiveness of the Mexica. This predatory Aztec tribe left the legendary city of Chicomoztoc and settled on an island in Lake Texcoco, site of modern Mexico City. Tenochtitlán, the Aztec capital, was founded here in A.D. 1325. For almost a century the Mexica remained the vassals of the Tepanecs of Atzacapotzalco and fought in their wars of conquest. In 1428, aided by the Acolhua of Texcoco, they defeated the Tepanecs and laid the foundations for the Aztec empire.

An Original Art Style : Aztec Palaces

Aztec leaders adopted a truly imperialistic foreign policy. They successively subdued the peoples of central Mexico: the Mixtecs and Zapotecs whose civilization was already on the wane. They then fought their way to the sea and defeated the Huastecs in the region of Tempico and the Totonacs in the modern state of Veracruz on the Gulf Coast. The Aztec realm extended from the Gulf of Mexico to the Pacific Ocean. It was the largest empire in pre-Columbian Mexico and covered an area greater than that of modern France. The Spanish Conquest in 1521 abruptly terminated Aztec expansion.

The pyramid of Tenayuca, capital of the Chichimecs, represents eight successive superimpositions. The structure was enlarged and embellished by the Aztecs in the fourteenth century.

Dedicated to Ehecatl, the Aztec wind-god, the round pyramid at Calixtlahuaca, near Toluca, represents four successive superimpositions. The last pyramid, almost entirely destroyed, has been eliminated by archaeologists.

During their 200 years long reign, the Aztecs succeeded in assimilating the cultural legacy of previous civilizations. They developed an art form founded mainly on Toltec traditions, characterized by austerity and geometric stylization.

Most of the secular architecture of the Aztec empire has been destroyed. Only meagre vestiges now remain. Cortés seized and plundared Tenochtitlán in 1521. Accounts written by his companions prove that Aztec palaces were enormous. The basic principle of construction was a square layout 200 m (660 ft.) on a side. Two- or three-storey buildings were erected round inner courtyards and patios. The upper level was reserved for the sovereign. The ground floor housed public offices: treasury, forum of justice, arsenals. The great assembly hall could seat 3,000 people. According to the accounts of the conquistadores, thirty horsemen could joust on the terrace!

Aztec palaces marked the highest development of the architectural concepts initiated at Tula and Chichén Itzá. The inner spaces created to meet new social and religious demands reached more gigantic dimensions than ever before.

Below:

Though the pre-Columbians never used wheeled vehicles for transporting building materials, this Aztec clay toy is mounted on four small wheels. (Museo Nacional de Antropología, Mexico City)

Under badly destroyed superstructures, Mexican archaeologists have discovered a small Aztec pyramid at Santa Cecilia, near Mexico City. The temple where human sacrifice took place is nearly intact.

Pyramids and Human Sacrifice

Aztec pyramids were known as "teocalli", or houses of the gods. They generally supported twin temples and were dedicated to two gods, for example Quetzalcóatl and his brother Tezcatlipoca, the two creator-gods of the Aztec pantheon. The Eagle and Jaguar, emblems of the armies and warrior fraternities, were supposed to feed the Sun, Huitzilopochtli — associated with Tlaloc, the rain-god — by means of human sacrifice. These sanguinary rites were performed on the raised platforms crowning the pyramids. Victims were immolated in order to preserve world order and encourage the Sun's return. Human hearts alone could satisfy the gods and sustain the sun in its daily orbit across the sky.

Some sort of death sacrifice existed in most Mesoamerican cultures as far back as the Preclassic period. Human sacrifice became however a

Below:

Aztec skull inlaid with jade and turquoise mosaic work. The eyes are pyrite spheres set in shell rings. This work of art was a present from Montezuma II to Cortés. The Aztecs seem to have been fascinated with death. (Museo Nacional de Antropología, Mexico City)

Aztec pyramid at the site of Teopanzolco, near Cuernavaca. The raised platform originally supported twin temples.

diagnostic trait of Aztec civilization. In 1488 at the dedication of the Great Pyramid of Tenochtitlán, Aztec priests sacrificed more than 20,000 captives.

Aztec temples and pyramids did not differ essentially from their Toltec prototypes. The pyramid was a raised platform constructed to support the temple. Superpositions were not infrequent (at Santa Cecilia for example archaeologists have discovered a perfectly well preserved pyramid under the ruins of a later monument). Sculptured decoration recalls Toltec architecture at Tulá.

Tenochtitlán under Montezuma II

The layout of Tenochtitlán must have been astonishing, if we are to believe the accounts of Spanish chroniclers contemporaneous with the Conquest. The sincere admiration voiced by Bernal Diaz del Castillo leads us to believe that the Aztec capital was a magnificent urban centre. According to these descriptions, the city resembled a New World Venice. Originally founded by the Mexica on an island in Lake Texcoco,

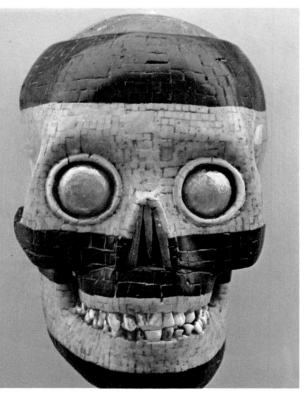

the city was laid out in a grid of streets and canals connected to the mainland by three great causeways. Each precinct was actually a separate islet. When the Europeans arrived, Tenochtitlán had already expanded beyond its original insular boundaries and the shores of the lake had also been built-up. All in all, the city probably covered an area of 1,000 hectares (2,500 acres). According to Ignacio Bernal, the total population amounted to at least 100,000. The Great Pyramid divided the town into four administrative districts.

Lake Texcoco was mostly saline. Two 5 km (3 mi.) long aqueducts were erected in order to supply the town with fresh water. Tenochtitlán was a city of parks and gardens. The houses were built round inner courts planted with trees.

The Aztec capital with its countless flat-roofed dwellings, whitewashed walls, green parks, canals, towering pyramids and raised temples, aqueducts and dikes — on which eight Spanish horsemen could ride abreast — must have been both picturesque and imposing. Tenochtitlán was truly a masterpiece of Mesoamerican town-planning. The conquistadores razed this splendid city to the ground. Its ruins underlie modern Mexico City. The arrival of the white man literally crushed the flourishing Aztec empire.

Exactly the same phenomenon occurred in South America when Pizarro landed in Peru. The Spaniards struck down the Inca empire at the height of its power.

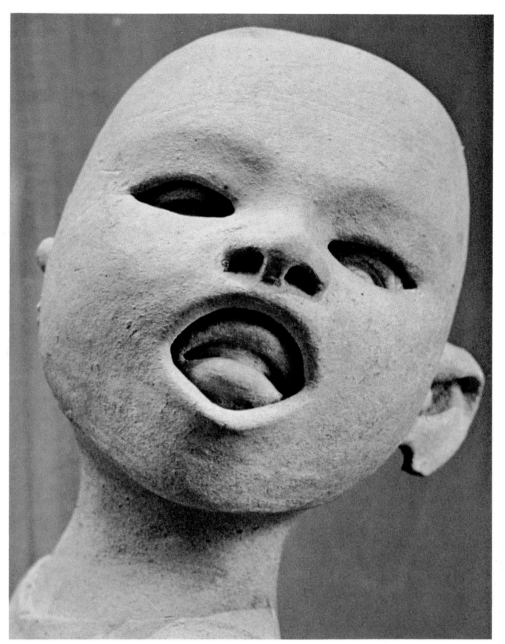

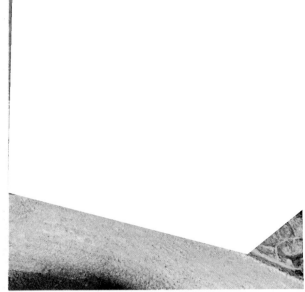

The God Xipe Totec worshipped by the Aztecs and the Totonacs was traditionally dressed in skins of flayed sacrificial victims.

Below:

The sanguinary rites of the Aztec religion were still performed at Malinalco several years after the Conquest. The ceremonial site is hidden in the mountains near Toluca. A thatched roof added by archaeologists re-creates the original appearance of the rock-cut shrine.

View of the Aztec temple at Malinalco. This shrine carved out of the living rock was dedicated to the warrior fraternities of Eagles and Jaguars.

Below:
The Chavín culture developed in the grandiose setting of the Andean Cordillera at the foot of a peak 6,000 m (19,700 ft.) high near the sources of the Marañón, tributary of the Amazon.

Pre-Inca Civilization in Peru

This werejaguar figure tenoned into the wall of the pyramid at Chavín watches over the earliest stone temple in pre-Columbian Peru.

In 1536 the Incas were defeated by a handful of Spaniards led by Pizarro. The most powerful Indian state in South America disappeared off the face of the earth. The Andean region including Peru and modern Bolivia became a Spanish colony. When we speak of Peru, we mean the area comprised within these original boundaries: a region extending from Ecuador to the Chilean border along a 2,500 km (1,550 mi.) stretch of the Pacific coast. The tremendous Andes mountain range cuts across the country from north to south. The mountain system splits up into several cordilleras, some of which reach a height of 6,000 m (19,700 ft.). The Andean area forms a complex pattern of ridges and V-shapped valleys separated by the high plateaux of the Altiplano at an altitude of nearly 4,000 m (13,000 ft.). To the east the surface slopes gently away toward the Amazon rain forest, never inhabited by the pre-Columbians...

Our knowledge of South American civilizations is extremely fragmentary and leaves much to be desried. Information is insufficient and many gaps have yet to be filled in. Relatively few excavations have been undertaken. Dating is unreliable. The treasures buried at archaeological sites have all too often attracted "huaqueros", or unauthorized pillagers. Museums and private collections the world over are full of works of art of unknown provenance and stratigraphy.

About 2500 B.C. the first agrarian communities settled in the highlands and the few valleys which connect the mountain ridges with the Pacific coast creating genuine oases amidst the dunes of the vast coastal deserts — among the most arid in the whole world. Corn (maize) was first cultivated about 1500 B.C. The earliest vestiges of pottery and weaving date back to the same period.

The Andean area is a geographic mosaic of many distinct niches. When highly developed civilizations finally replaced primitive societies, these various regions isolated by desert and mountain spurs gave birth to extremely divergent cultures. The evolution of Andean civilization extended over a period of two thousand years. In order to simplify our task, we shall divide this evolution into two separate zones: the north and the south. Few pre-Inca civilizations exerted a culturally unifying influence on the region.

Chavín Culture

In Peru, as in Preclassic Mexico, the earliest phases of cultural development have left no vestiges. The most ancient monuments bearing witness to the existence of a highly developed civilization date back to about 850–500 B.C.
Stone architecture first appeared at the site of Chavín, on the eastern

The site of Chavín: a pyramid with walls of coursed masonry supported twin temples dedicated to the Condor and Jaguar. This structure was built about 500 B.C.

Snake-haired werejaguar god worshipped at Chavín.

69

stope of the Andes, situated in a high valley on a tributary of the Marañón, east of the Callejón de Huaylas.

In order to reach the site, one must go through the town of Huaraz recently ravaged by a terrible earthquake. Chavín is located in the very heart of the Andes. Glaciers overlook the deep narrow valley. Chavín seems to have been an important religious centre, the jaguar being the chief object of worship. The structures built on the valley floor are clustered about a central plaza 50 m (164 ft.) on a side. The complex also includes a nearly square platform known as the Castillo, 72 m (236 ft.) long, 70 m (230 ft.) wide and 13 m (43 ft.) high, which originally supported two edifices now badly destroyed.

The stone platforms are formed of rubble faced by walls of coursed masonry. The walls are decorated at equidistant intervals with odd werejaguar heads carved in the round. On the southern façade two stairways lead up to twin temples. Paired columns rise up in front of the gate which gives access to the stairways.

The structures are honeycombed with galleries running parallel to the walls at different levels and ventilated by shafts. The result is a complicated network of underground passageways. A strange sculpture 4.5 m (15 ft.) high stands at the crossing of a cruciform gallery. "El Lanzón" is a monolithic effigy of the werejaguar god whose secret shrine was probably hidden here in the heart of the structure.

In the middle of the first millenium B.C. the Chavín art style spread over a large part of pre-Columbian Peru. Characterized by an extremely elaborate stylization, it by no means recalls "primitive" art forms. It indeed seems to be the result of a long evolution, though we know nothing of its early beginnings. Perhaps the first cultural phases produced wooden sculptures and monuments which have not been preserved. In that case, the sculptures found at Chavín can be regarded as mere petrifications, i.e. stone copies of earlier works of art. The use of imputrescible materials marked the ultimate phase of the Chavín culture.

The Pyramid of the Moon is the most prominent monument in the town of Moche located in the coastal plain.

Facing page, above:
Stylized statue visibly influenced by the Chavín art style.

Facing page, below:
Two carved stelae found at the site of Cerro Sechín on the Pacific coast. The twelve severed heads incised on the stela to the right represent perhaps the skulls of sacrificial victims.

Moche stirrup-spouted pots exhibit a highly realistic style. This musician wrapped in aponchc and wearing a pointed hat seems almost alive. (Lima Museum)

71

The extraordinary variety of expressions depicted by Moche potters includes the fearful grin of death as well as the serene face of a wealthy merchant. These ceramic figural sculptures recall the art styles of western Mexico. (Lima Museum)

On the Pacific coast, far from the high mountains, the site of Cerro Sechín in the Casma Valley also exhibits sculptured stelae. Though lacking Chavín characteristics, they may be contemporaneous with the works discovered at the site of Chavín. These flat stones with naturalistic incised designs showing standing men carrying clubs recall the low-reliefs decorating the palace of the "Danzantes" at Monte Albán in Mexico. Aesthetic standards are quite similar. These low-reliefs have led to conjectures about a possible Mesoamerican influence on Peruvian art...

In the Huaraz Valley near Chavín a somewhat later, ill-known culture has left odd egg-shaped adobe sculptures depicting stylized squatting figures. They are perhaps three-dimensional portraits of the important dead. At the same site archaeologists have excavated lithic tombs. Drystone construction recalls the prehistoric technique of the Nuraghes in Sardinia or the Boriies in Provence.

These art forms may seem eccentric and incongruous. In actual fact, they developed over a period of a thousand years. Divergent styles reflect the isolation of the various regions cut off from one another by mountain ridges. Nonetheless, pottery techniques bear witness to a

Chan Chan, the capital of the powerful Chimú realm, flourished about A.D. 1000 in the coastal plain at the foot of the Andes. The town was entirely built of adobe. Most structures are now badly destroyed.

In some parts of Chan Chan archaeologists have undertaken to restore walls offwering decorative motifs.

74

common source of inspiration. Stirrup-spouted bottles have been found at Chavín as well as at Moche, Nazca and Chimú sites. This form was in vogue in the whole of Peru for over two thousand years.

Classic Moche Culture

Pottery was one of the chief modes of artistic expression in ancient Peru. Classic Moche culture began to flourish in the second century and continued through the seventh century of the Christian era. The Moche art style was highly naturalistic and much different from the complex stylization in vogue at Chavín. Designs generally represent scenes from everyday life. Portraits, caricatures and humorous erotic scenes decorate admirable polychrome pots moulded in forms that include figures, animals, plants and weapons. The potter's wheel was unknown at Moche. Some pots have moulded designs in low relief. Details were retouched before the clay hardened.

The inhabitants of the Moche Valley on the northern coast of Peru had a highly organized society made possible by intensive irrigation. Their irrigation system included constructions which still fill us with

Aerial view of the Chimú capital with its ten large rectangular enclosures. This central area, known as the "Labyrinth", can be divided into two zones, one containing dwelling-places and storehouses, the other one forming a vast plaza with two adobe pyramids damaged byu treasure-hunters. The enclosure is 530 m (1,740 ft.) long and 265 m (870 ft.) wide.

admiration. Canals no less than 130 km (80 mi.) long brought water from the mountains to the coastal plain and encouraged the development of a prosperous agrarian economy. These canals, parts of which are made up of aqueducts resembling adobe dikes, cross over ravines 20 m (66 ft.) deep and nearly 1,500 m (4,900 ft.) long. They are among the most impressive achievements of Andean civilization. Some were still in use in the early twentieth century.

The Moche culture is also remarkable for its architectural achievements. One of the most imposing monuments is the Huaca de la Luna at Moche. This palace is built on a terrace 250 m (820 ft.) long, 150 m (490 ft.) wide and 20 m (66 ft.) high facing a pyramid known as the Huaca del Sol (the site was dedicated to the sun by the Incas). The Pyramid of the Sun is a square structure 110 m (360 ft.) on a side and 25 m (82 ft.) high. More than a million cubic metres of adobe were used in its construction. The waters of the Moche River have considerably eroded the structure.

According to early seventeenth century sources, the Spaniards who excavated the necropolis at Moche discovered a veritable treasure of artifacts of gold, precious stones and ceramics. As far back as the Classic period the techniques of goldwork (cire perdue casting, wire drawing, repoussé work, embossing and soldering) were highly developed. Moche goldsmiths executed high-quality works for religious purposes. Many such ornaments were placed in the tombs of important dignitaries.

The Fantastic Chimú Capital

An immense city known as Chan Chan rises up on the coast not far from Moche. Its colossal dimensions — it covers an area of over 28 square kilometres (11 square miles) — and odd layout — the central area contains a series of walled precincts, or "palaces" forming rectangular enclosures the largest of which is 530 m (1,740 ft.) long and 265 m (870 ft.) wide — make the Chimú capital the most important pre-Columbian metropolis in South America.

Chimú expansion began about the twelfth century A.D. The Chimú are generally considered to be the precursors of the Incas who learned a great deal from them. According to traditions recorded shortly after the Spanish Conquest, the Chimú had their homeland in the north. They came to the Moche Valley by sea on balsa rafts. The Chimú had a powerful, aggressive organized state. It was actually a confederation of

Two chased gold plume holders found in the Ica Valley, viewed in profile and full-face. They are 7 cm (2 ³/₄ in.) high. (Musée d'Ethnographie, Geneva)

Above:

Chased gold brassard found in the Ica Valley. The conquistadores who conquered Peru were greedly for gold. (Musée d'Ethnographie, Geneva)

Facing page, above:

Stylized chased gold death mask. (Musée d'Ethnographie, Geneva)

Chimú chased gold death mask. (Musée d'Ethnographie, Geneva)

Inca gold llama, 5 cm (2 in.) high. (Musée d'Ethnographie, Geneva)

Above right:
Chimú tweezers. (Musée d'Ethnographie, Geneva)

Cast-gold Inca figurines. (Musée d'Ethnographie, Geneva)

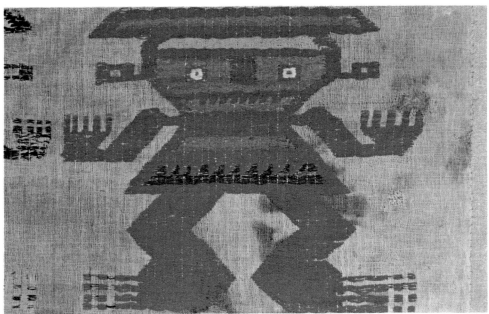

Shroud found at Paracas: javelin-bearers with serpentiform headdresses. Parrots are embroidered on either side of the main figures. (Fondation Abegg, Bern)

Above right:

Chimú textile fragment showing an extremely stylized human figure. (Fondation Abegg, Bern)

Right:

Shroud found at Paracas representing a human figure carrying a severed head and a javelin. (Fondation Abegg, Bern)

Facing page, above:

Chimú-style feather poncho. Few such feather mosaics have been preserved. All have been found at sites in the coastal deserts. (Fondation Abegg, Bern)

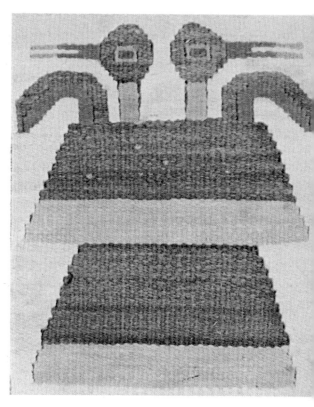

Chimú textile fragment showing two storks in their nest. (Fondation Abegg, Bern)

Below left:
Nazca textile band: warriors armed with javelins. (Fondation Abegg, Bern)

Below center:
Paracas textile fragment: falling figure. (Fondation Abegg, Bern)

Paracas textile fragment: diving bird. (Fondation Abegg, Bern)

city-states similar to the system developed by the Moche culture five hundred years before. In order to unify the country the Chimú created a network of roads and a system of official communication.

The Chimú drew heavily on Moche traditions. Their achievements in the field of metallurgy were particularly outstanding. A genuine advance technology metallurgical industry seems to have existed in the Chimú capital. The works of art produced are remarkable for their high quality and colossal dimensions. The conquistadores described enormous gold and silver vessels large enough to contain a quartered ox, sacrificial tables, panels and temple doors several metres on a side all in one piece. Chimú metalwork including death masks, sacrificial knives, jewelled ornaments and pectorals was mythicized by the Spaniards, fascinated by the legend of El Dorado.

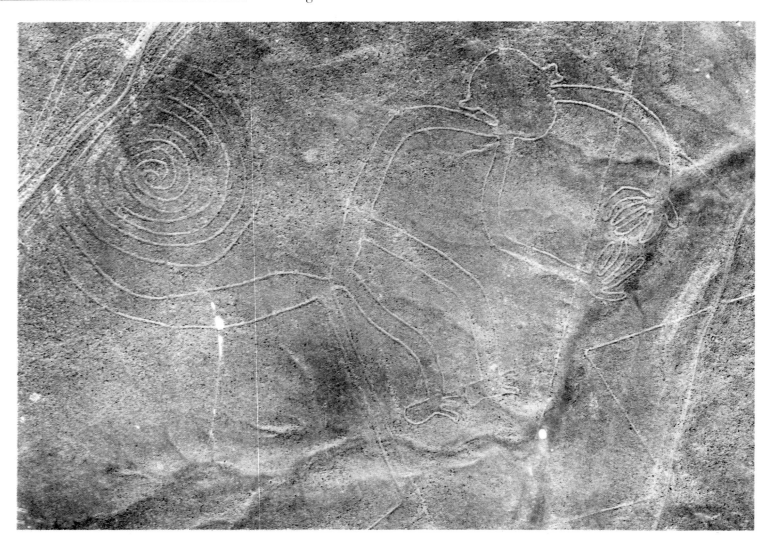

The gigantic figures drawn by the Nazcas in the coastal deserts of Peru are one of the great mysteries of the pre-Columbian world. This odd monkey several dozen metres long is a continuous-line drawing.

Above:
Nazca ceramic bowl. Nazca art, less naturalistic than Moche pottery, is characterized by its varied colouring and highly formal designs.

Facing page:
The great Condor drawn by the Nazcas has a 120 m (394 ft.) wingspan.

Town-planning at Chan Chan reflected the strictly hierarchic organization of Chimú society. The city built on the sea-coast was composed of large rectangular enclosures covering an area of about ten hectares (25 acres) each. These minicities, sometimes called ciudadelas, were probably inhabited by different social classes and trades. They were surrounded by tapering adobe walls which reach a height of ten metres (33 ft.). Each enclosure contained stores, workshops and dwelling-places. A pyramid rose up in the middle of the religious precinct. Town streets were arranged in a rectangular pattern.

The Gorgeous Textiles of Paracas

The climate of the Peruvian Pacific coast — especially in the south — is extremely dry. The admirable shrouds in which the inhabitants of Paracas buried their dead have therefore come down to us intact.

Archaeologists led by Julio Tello who also directed excavations at Chavín, discovered a great number of tombs on this wind-swept sandy promontory. These tombs date from about 350 B.C. to A.D. 200.

These sepulchres contained textiles so well preserved that they seem brand new, though they are actually over two thousand years old. The textiles were generally found in the mummy bundles of the important dead. Some of these sumptuous burial robes are 2.5 m (8.2 ft.) long and 1.5 m (4.9 ft.) wide.

The shrouds found at Paracas are especially remarkable for their vivid colours — burgundy, brick-red, orange, yellow and red ochre. They display a surprisingly wide range of weaving techniques including tapestry and embroidery. The result is a very complicated and somewhat conventionalized design. Human figures, deities and mythological animals such as the Jaguar and the Serpent-Dragon are depicted on a solid or chequered background.

These brilliant weaving techniques were handed down to later Peruvian civilizations: the Nazca culture, the Chimú and even the Incas.

Nazca : Gigantic Drawings in the Desert

A style of pottery very different from that of the Moche culture developed about A.D. 350–850 south of Paracas in the Nazca region. This fine polychrome pottery is much less naturalistic than contemporaneous Moche works. The colours most often used are mauve and purple, garnet red and yellow ochre. A sharp-cut black or white linear design enhances the beauty of the finished work. Geometric stylization and economy of line result in an austere and elegant perfection.

The Nazca culture flourished on the edge of the coastal deserts of southern Peru. This pre-Columbian civilization has left colossal drawings traced on the ground in the arid region extending from the foothills of the Cordillera to a range of hills sheltering the plain from sea-side sandstorms. Earth banks form gigantic figures and geometric designs covering a zone 70 km (44 mi.) long. Some of these drawings are simple straight lines running across hills and dales over a distance of almost 8 km (5 mi.). Others represent stylized life forms: birds, monkeys, fish, spiders, flowers, etc.

Some of these drawings reach a length of several dozen metres. They are invisible from the ground. They were discovered thanks largely to aerial photographs taken in oblique light. The lines are actually shallow furrows ploughed in the rocky soil. Since it hardly ever rains in the region, these frail designs made fifteen centuries ago have come down to us nearly intact.

What was the purpose of these gigantic drawings in the middle of the desert? How could they be made, since they cannot be seen from the

Carved stela found at Tiahuanaco representing Viracocha, the creator-god. The city of Tiahuanaco flourished from A.D. 600 to 1200. Tiahuanaco art is characterized by austere stylization.

Up to the present the Uru tribe still lives on the shores of Lake Titicaca. These Indians are fishermen who live on reed islets, dwell in reed huts, sail in reed skiffs and catch fish in reed traps. In short, a very primitive reed-age culture...

82

ground ? These questions and many others puzzle archaeologists. Perhaps the straight lines indicated astronomical observations or sighting lines. The figures may in that case have stood for the various constellations or signs of the zodiac used for calendrical computations. The lines may have been drawn by means of ropes stretched along the ground. The drawings may have necessitated the use of enormous kites strong enough to lift up a full-grown man. Be that as it may, these vast drawings — such as the Great Condor with its 120 m (394 ft.) wing-span — bear witness to an unmastered technical skill. The drawing is made up of one continuous line which seems indeed to have been traced with the help of a compass. They are now thought to be sun paths. By following a certain line at the equinox or solstice, one can see the sun rising or setting on the horizon straight ahead.

Were these drawing meant to be seen by the gods ? Much ink has been

Ruins of the ancient city of Tiahuanaco: rows of remarkable carved monoliths.

Left:

Two sculptures found at Tiahuanaco. One has highly stylized features. The other one is slightly more naturalistic.

Right:

Geometric stylization of the sculpture depicting the god Viracocha on the Gate of the Sun at Tiahuanaco.

Detail of a funerary tower, or Chullpa, on the shore of Lake Sillustani. The walls are of tightly-jointed coursed masonry.

The highland culture which built the Chullpas flourished from the fall of Tiahuanaco in the twelfth century to the beginning of Inca expansion in the fifteenth century. Many such funerary towers rise up at the site of Sillustani near Lake Titicaca.

spilt about this question which has yet received no satisfactory answer. Some science-fiction fanatics have asserted that Nazca drawings were "landing strips for interplanetary space-ships"...

Tiahuanaco, a Highland Sanctuary

About A.D. 600–1200 an important civilization arose in the south highlands (modern Bolivia) on the shores of Lake Titicaca at an altitude of 3,800 metres (12,500 ft.). Their religious capital was Tiahuanaco. Thiahuanaco subjugated the surrounding realms and assumed dominion over a large part of the country before the rise of the Incas. Sensation-mongers have made all kinds of far-fetched hypotheses about this highland civilization. They trace back its origins to legendary times hundreds of thousands of years gone by! They say the city was flooded by a 5,000 m (16,400 ft.) high apocalyptic tidal wave.

Tiahuanaco architecture exhibits the same basic characteristics as the nomumental structures erected at Chavín. Platforms are formed of rubble faced by walls of coursed masonry. The walls are decorated with low-reliefs. Subject matter and stylization recall the decoration of the

Castillo at Chavín. We see the same austere symbolism characterized by bold, symmetric designs; the same profusion of mythological animals such as serpents, jaguars, condors. The aesthetic affinity between these two sites leads us to believe that a cultural bridge must have joined the two cultures separated by a distance of 1,300 km (800 mi.), in spite of the fact that the Chavín culture disappeared in the first century B.C. long before the rise of Tiahuanaco (about A.D. 250).

At the site of Tiahuanaco proper several architectural complexes composed of enormous monolithic doorways can still be seen. They are however badly destroyed since the ancient ceremonial centre was long used as a quarry during the construction of modern La Paz. Besides the famous Gate of the Sun, a vast plaza recalls the sculptured decoration peculiar to Chavín. Stone heads are tenoned into the walls. The monolithic doorways composed of large carved panels are cut from

gigantic blocks of lava. We can also see sculptured columns resembling the Atlantean roof-supports at Tula in Mexico. These 7 m (23 ft.) high statues are among the largest sculptured monoliths discovered in South America.

After the fall of Tiahuanaco, a later highland civilization (subsequently swallowed up by the Inca empire) built structures known as Chullpa. These funerary structures resembling round towers rise up on the shore of Lake Sillustani, north of Lake Titicaca. These tombs probably date back to the thirteenth and fourteenth centuries.

In the southern coastal region the Chincha realm centred in the Inca Valley near Nazca effected the transition between Tiahuanaco and the Incas. This highly developed civilization, famous for its weaving and goldwork, was annexed by the Inca empire in 1476.

Lake Sillustani located at an altitude of 4,000 m (13,000 ft.) is one of the most beautiful sites in the Peruvian highlands.

The Collectivist Inca Empire

Like the Aztecs, the Incas who developed the last great culture in Peru before the Spanish Conquest were a warlike people who had their homeland in a region of high plateaux. They formed their tremendous empire by conquering and subjugating more than 100 independent ethnic groups. About A.D. 1000 the Incas, natives of the region extending from Lake Titicaca to Huari, settled in the Cuzco Valley where they founded their capital.

The Inca empire was the result of two hundred years of unceasing struggles. The great wars of conquest began in 1438 during the reign of Pachacuti Inca Yupanqui. The Inca state rapidly expanded beyond its original highland boundaries and soon extended from Ecuador on the north to Chile on the south. Once they had gained a firm hold over the mountains, they set upon the task of subjugating the coastal regions. Though the ethnic groups settled in the coastal plains unquestionably had a more highly developed civilization, they were also extremely vulnerable. These essentially agrarian societies were wholly dependent on their irrigation system. The Incas who controlled the high mountain valleys diverted rivers and streams by means of canals, cut off the water supply and took hold of the coastal realms.

By means of a cunning policy of aggression, intimidation and persuasion, the Incas annexed the powerful Chimú state about 1450. Chimú influence is visible in almost all aspects of Inca civilization. The Incas drew heavily on their new vassals in the fields of town-planning and metallurgy. They deported the entire population of Chan Chan to their mountainous homeland. Forced resettlement was indeed one of the chief means used by the Incas to subdue newly conquered provinces and guarantee obedience to the state.

A street in Cuzco, the capital of the Inca empire. The walls are of magnificent coursed masonry. After the Conquest, Spanish colonists increased the height of the walls and added baroque doorways.

Megalithic bastion at Ollantaytambo. Colossal stone blocks were fashioned with such tight-fitting joints that no mortar was needed to hold them together.

Thanks to these brutal yet efficacious tactics, the Inca realm soon became the biggest empire in the New World. At the end of the fifteenth century Topa Inca Yupanqui ruled over a country twice as large as modern France. At the height of its power, the Inca empire extended from Quito to Talca south of Santiago — a distance of 4,000 km (2,500 mi.) from north to south.

The Organization of the Empire

This tremendous empire was governed by the Inca who ruled by divine right and claimed lineal descent from the gods. The sun and the moon were believed to be the ruler's ancestors. The monarch himself was worshipped as divine during his lifetime. In addition, he was generalissimo, high priest and "head of state". He delegated limited powers to his close relatives. When territorial expansion made this system impossible, talented "noblemen" were also named to high offices and sent to fill responsible administrative positions in the provinces. Their rank was however lower than that of the Inca's close relatives.

In the Rimac Valley near Lima an Inca town built of rammed earth and adobe has been completely restored. These fortified pre-Columbian haciendas are remarkable for their modern layout and well defined volumes.

Detail of the storied ornamentation of a wooden cup ("kero") dating from the late Inca period or the first years of the Conquest. (Lima Museum)

Partial view of the triple ramparts at Sac-sahuaman overlooking Cuzco. This colossal bastion is a masterpiece of Inca architecture. Built in the late fifteenth century, it is over 500 m (1,640 ft.) long.

The members of this elite alone were granted certain privileges. They alone could own land. The rest of the population (which may well have amounted to a total of seven million) was classified into age-grades (a person was taxed according to his age) and decimal units of 10, 50, 100, 500, 1,000, 5,000 and 10,000 taxpayers administered by the kurakas. This system made it easier to collect the labour taxes owed to the ruler. The pasture lands, llama and alpaca herds, cocoa plantations and mines were owned and managed by the government. One third of the land was the property of the Inca, one third was the property of the state religion. The remainder of the harvest was distributed among the peasants who tilled the soil.

Provisions were stocked in enormous warehouses controlled by the government. Famines were unknown in the Inca empire. The state also owned and controlled the means of exchange; trade was brought under strict regulation.

Power was concentrated in the hands of the absolute ruler. Although the Inca was god and high priest all in one, he did not compel conquered groups to give up their own religious beliefs. As long as his subjects agreed to worship the sun, Inti, ancestor of the Inca, they were also allowed to worship the "huacas", or idols as they were called by the Christians. The two chief gods of the Inca empire were Inti and

Viracocha, the creatorgod. Human sacrifice was almost as common as in the Aztec religion. When the Inca died, priests immolated thousands of women and servants who were supposed to attend on him in the nether world.

The Road System and the Technics

A remarkable network of roads made it possible to govern such a large area from a single capital. A similar network had already been created by the Moche confederation and the Chimú realm. The Incas further extended and rigorously organized the existent system which became a tool of their imperialism. Road-makers took into account the lie of the land. One of the main arteries runs along the coast from Tumbez on the north all the way to Chile. The highland road runds parallel to the coastal road from Ecuador to Argentina. A network of smaller, lateral roads join these two great highways and connect the coastal region with the Altiplano. On the whole, the network included some 15,000 km (9,300 mi.) of roads.

In flat open country Inca roads are 8 m (26 ft.) wide but they grow much narrower in the mountain passes. Here and there the roadway is replaced by a stairway hewn out of the rock. In the high cols tunnels

Detail of the storied ornamentation of an Inca "kero" cup showing llamas.

Above:

Llama herd in front of the colossal ramparts at Sacsahuaman. The walls are built of enormous stone blocks weighing several tons each.

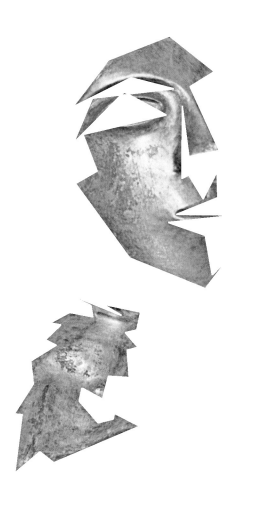

have been driven through the mountain. Wooden or stone cantilever bridges cross over the ravines. We can also see genuine suspension bridges with cables made of braided aloe fibre. One of these suspension bridges, 60 m (197 ft.) long, was still used in the nineteenth century. It was built in 1350 over a gorge in the Apurimac. The cables were as thick as a man's thigh.

A maintenance staff kept the roads in repair. Paved causeways were built across marshes. Along the coast low drystone walls prevented the roads from being buried under desert sands. The Indians had no wheeled vehicles. The roads were used by pedestrians, litter-bearers and llama caravans. The llama, the only pack animal known in South America before the Conquest, could carry only 40 kg (88 lbs.). Runners stationed in relays conveyed the ruler's orders. These royal messengers could cover a distance of 700 km (435 mi.) in four days. The relays, or tampos, also served as shelters and storehouses and were located at one-day intervals along all of the roads.

The Inca empire made no real innovations. The Incas were most remarkable for their prodigious sense of organization. They created a socialist system in which the state owned and controlled the means of production, distribution and exchange. Private initiative and discoveries were encouraged. The Inca empire was moreover characterized by a cultural syncretism; Chimú, Moche and Nazca influences converged at Cuzco.

In the field of metallurgy, the Incas popularized the use of bronze tools and weapons. Bronze had been invented by the Chimú but it did not come into general use before the rise of the Inca empire. Gold and silver — symbols of the sun and the moon — still played a very important part in religious ceremonies. When Atahuallpa was kidnapped by the Spaniards, Pizarro demanded a ransom including several cubic metres of gold plate and gold and silver statues and ornaments...

The taxes levied by the ruler were generally paid in kind or in the form of labour. Coins were unknown. The Incas were the first people in the New World to invent the equal-arm balance, used for weighing various commodities. Tax collectors also used a kind of adding machine ("quipu") consisting of a main cord and a variable number of pendant cords of different colours. Knots denoted units, tens, hundreds and thousands. The Incas had a decimal system like our own. The quipu was a mnemonic device similar to the abacus. It was also used for conveying "coded" messages. The Incas never developed a written language.

Architectural Achievements

The principal manifestation of Inca genius for organization is the immense collective effort which gave birth to the structures known as "andenes" which still strike all those who travel in the high valleys of Peru. The "andenes" are terraces contrived on the mountainside. They made agriculture possible in the highlands. Tens of thousands of kilometres of retaining walls were built on the steep slopes of the Andes. Entire mountainsides have been transformed into networks of terraced fields where Indian peasants cultivated corn (maize) and other food crops. Even in the most secluded valleys we can still see vestiges of this tremendous undertaking. The Incas actually reshaped their environment in order to make the most of what nature had given them. The drystone retaining walls are still standing, though the mountains have lost their population and the fields have been abandoned.

Inca architecture borrowed heavily from the city of Tiahuanaco. Unlike the adobe structures erected in the coastal plains, early highland cities were built entirely of stone.

Oddly enough, in spite of their genius for organization the layout of the first towns built by the Incas was rather nondescript. Their capital, Cuzco, does not have a strict geometric layout. The town is divided into precincts, but the configuration of the ground alone accounts for the alignment of its winding streets. The walls of the palaces and temples are all of magnificent coursed masonry.

When the Incas took possession of the coastal plains, they adopted the building techniques of the peoples they conquered. Cities like Viracocha Pampa were built of adobe bricks. Streets were arranged in a rectangular pattern and met at right angles. The layout of public squares, warehouses, dwelling-places and palaces recalls Chimú town-planning. The same holds true for the town of Pikillacta. Like Viracocha Pampa, Pikillacta is characterized by a vast central plaza surrounded by a grid of streets meeting at right angles.

The same building techniques and overall plan also characterized smaller constructions such as the Inca towns recently restored in the Rimac Valley near Lima. These vast pre-Columbian "haciendas" were

Facing page, above:
The city-fortress of Pisac overlooking the Urubamba Valley. In the foreground, the temple complex and upper part of the town. To the left one can see the semicircular lower part of the town built at the edge of the cliff.

Facing page, below:
Inca silver female figurine. These statuettes were perhaps votive offerings. They were generally dressed in vividly coloured robes. (Lima Museum)

Terraced fields near Pisac. These andenes built on the steep slopes of the Andes covered a large part of the Peruvian highlands in the time of the Incas.

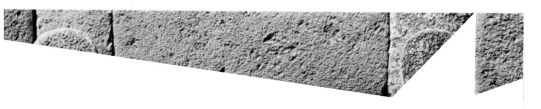

Detail of the admirable coursed masonry of a temple at Pisac. The trapezoidal window and protruding corbels are characteristic of late Inca architecture.

91

probably the centre of rural estates. They are remarkable for their modern layout, well defined volumes, flat roofs, inclined ramps and shady colonnades.

The Creations of the Central Region

The most outstanding achievements of Inca architects can be seen at Cuzco and in the surrounding area. The fortress of Sacsahuaman overlooking the capital is built of cyclopean blocks of stone the largest of which are 7 m (23 ft.) high and weigh over 100 tons. The triple ramparts adorned with redans are 540 m (1,870 ft.) round. These walls rising tier upon tier reach a height of 19 m (62 ft.). The rampart originally sheltered a "castle" complete with dwelling-places, warehouses and reservoirs now razed to the ground. This tremendous stronghold was erected about 1493 during the reign of Topa Inca Yupanqui. Thirty thousand workmen were probably employed at the building site.

In the town of Ollantaytambo built on both banks of the Patacancha River, we find another remarkable bastion with walls of mortarless masonry. Stones weighing several tons were fashioned with such tight-fitting joints that no mortar was needed to hold them together. The Incas had neither cranes nor wheeled vehicles. According to specialists, these enormous blocks of stone were probably moved out on rollers and ramps.

The town of Pisac, a genuine eagle's nest surrounded by andenes overlooking the gorges of the Urubamba Valley, has a very complicated layout. The town is made up of a semicircular lower part and a fortified upper part containing a complex of temples and palaces. All of the edifices are built of coursed masonry. The style is extremely simple.

The fantastic Inca fortress of Machu Picchu is also built on the Urubamba downstream from Pisac. Discovered in 1911 by the American explorer Hiram Bingham, this city-fortress escaped notice when the Spaniards invaded the country. Machu Picchu is built on a ridge

between two peaks which rise up perpendicularly on three sides so as to form a natural fortress hemmed in by a bend of the river and invisible from the valley floor.

In this wild and grandiose setting, an entire city complete with habitation-sites, enclosure walls, temples and an open-air altar for sacrifices lay buried under rank jungle overgrowth. It has now been restored. The buildings were all intact except for the timber work and thatched roofs which had rotted away. Machu Picchu gives us an idea of the life of an Inca garrison in an outpost of the Amazon basin. The Incas had entered into relations with the inhabitants of the Amazon rain forest who sold them precious wood and gold dust.

At Machu Picchu we find once more the megalithic coursed masonry, the austere simplicity and the trapezoidal openings characteristic of sixteenth century Inca architecture. The Spanish Conquest put an end to the art style, remarkable techniques and fascinating organization of the Inca empire. With the help of a few horses, two small canons and a dozen muskets, less than two hundred Europeans crushed the most powerful civilization of the pre-Columbian world.

Facing page :
The stone of sacrifice overlooking the town of Machu Picchu resembles an abstract sculpture.

A particularly interesting structure at Machu Picchu displays a massive cross wall which originally supported the roof frame.

Above left :

Andenes climbing the mountainside at Machu Picchu. The Inca outpost is perched at the summit of nearly perpendicular cliffs.

Andenes at the entrance to the town of Machu Picchu. Thatched roofs have been added to some buildings which thus look exactly the same as when they housed an Inca garrison five hundred years ago.

Photo credits

The 180 colour photographs that illustrate this work were all provided by Henri Stierlin, Geneva, except for the following documents:
Yvan Butler, Geneva, p. 9 below right, 17, 24 above right, 24-25, 25 above right, 29 right, 30, 36 right, 42 below, 44 above left, 47 above right, 60, 61 above left and below, 70 below, 71, 72, 73, 74, 86, 87 below, 88, 89, 90 below, 92, 95 below.
Roland Burkhard, Geneva, p. 10-11.
The author and photographer is most grateful to all those who made this book possible: the Oaxaca Regional Museum, Museo Nacional de Antropología (Mexico City), Palenque Museum, Villahermosa Open-air Museum, Lima Museum, Musée d'Ethnographie (Geneva), Fondation Abegg (Riggisberg, Bern).